Walter Tetley

For Corn's Sake

Walter Tetley

For Corn's Sake

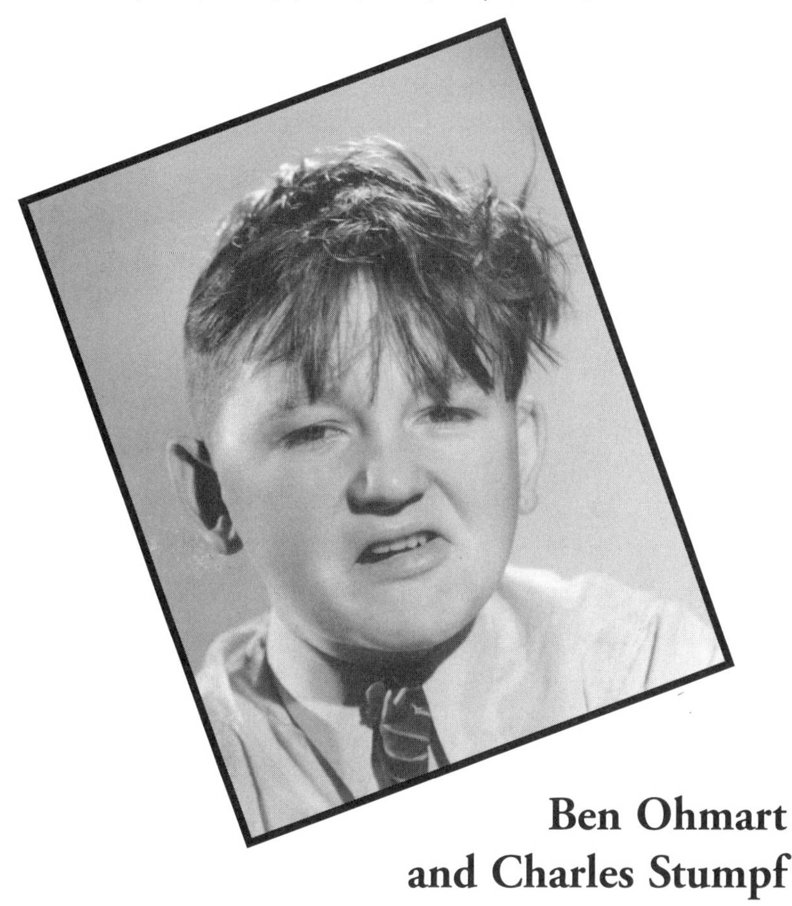

Ben Ohmart
and Charles Stumpf

BearManor Media
2003

Walter Tetley: For Corn's Sake

Published in the USA by

BearManor Media
P. O. Box 750
Boalsburg, PA 16827

bearmanormedia.com

Cover design by John Teehan
Typesetting and layout by John Teehan

ISBN—1-59393-000-3

Table of Contents

Foreword

There are very few today who remember the name of Walter Tetley. Some early TV fans may remember him as "Sherman," the fresh-faced, bespectacled "pet boy" of "Peabody," a talking white beagle who also wore glasses and a red bow-tie, and lived in a penthouse. Peabody had invented the "Way-Back Machine" in which the peculiar pair traveled through time and space, and got involved in all sorts of misadventures throughout history. It was an animated cartoon series that aired as a segment of the *Rocky and His Friends* show. Tetley supplied the voice for Sherman in all 91 episodes of *Peabody's Improbable History.*

Other older fans who can recall the golden age of radio should remember several of Tetley's other outstanding roles—as Leroy, the wisecracking nephew of The Great Gildersleeve, and as the tough-talking delivery boy, Julius Abbruzio, on *The Phil Harris/Alice Faye Show.*

Early in his career Walter worked with Fred Allen who considered him an eminently skilled comedian to be reckoned with. He also worked on other highly rated radio comedy shows with Jack Benny, George Burns and Gracie Allen, and Joe Penner. Walter skillfully played dramatic roles on classic shows such as *Cavalcade of America, Lux Radio Theater* and *Suspense.* He also had regular roles on continuing radio shows such as *Buck Rogers*. In addition, he gave voice to "Tigger" on a radio version of *Winnie the Pooh*, as well as the role of "Tip" in a serialization of *The Wizard of Oz.*

Tetley's radio career began in 1930 when he made weekly appearances on children's shows—*The Children's Hour* and *The Lady Next Door*—doing his remarkable impersonation of legendary Scottish entertainer, Sir Harry Lauder.

He gained renown for his precise comedy timing and sure-fire delivery, getting every possible nuance out of every line. Walter held his own while sharing the microphone with such show business legends as the Barrymores and Helen Hayes.

Very little is known of the actor's private life. It is recalled that he had the epitome of all stage mothers, who practically thrust him into the lucrative limelight. He magically managed to sound like a 12-year-old throughout his many years on radio and in voice-over work. He was a very private person and rarely granted interviews. Former co-workers recall his selfless nature and his utter lack of conceit.

Part of the mystery was unraveled when scrapbooks of his early career, that had been kept by his parents, were located. Also a wealth of information was found in a little black notebook that his father kept, listing each one of the auditions, broadcasts and personal appearances that Walter made. These records provided much of the information found in these pages. You can read more about it in the "How This Book Came To Be" at the end.

Memories fade and die, and if history is not passed on by the printed page, even the greatest personalities can be lost to the world. From Walter's scrapbooks and the little black notebook, we have pieced together as much of the story as possible. We located a few of the people he worked with, but there was little they could tell us. If there is anyone out there who can possibly help fill in the gaps, please get in touch.

Walter Tetley was a very big part of radio. He made us laugh, and he must be remembered. Who could ever forget that voice?

The Authors
September 2003

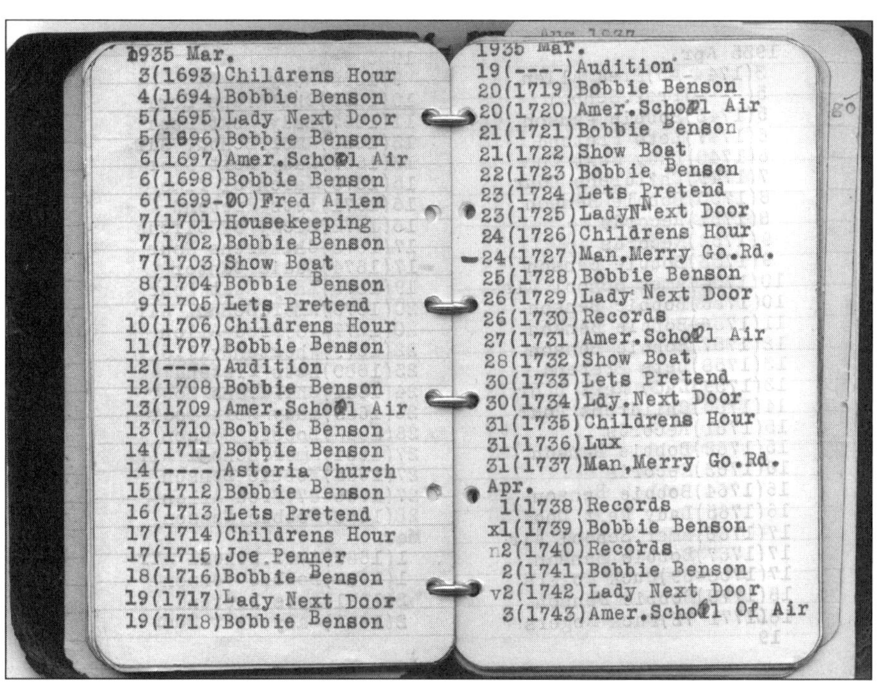

1935 Mar.
3(1693)Childrens Hour
4(1694)Bobbie Benson
5(1695)Lady Next Door
5(1696)Bobbie Benson
6(1697)Amer.School Air
6(1698)Bobbie Benson
6(1699-00)Fred Allen
7(1701)Housekeeping
7(1702)Bobbie Benson
7(1703)Show Boat
8(1704)Bobbie Benson
9(1705)Lets Pretend
10(1706)Childrens Hour
11(1707)Bobbie Benson
12(----)Audition
12(1708)Bobbie Benson
13(1709)Amer.School Air
13(1710)Bobbie Benson
14(1711)Bobbie Benson
14(----)Astoria Church
15(1712)Bobbie Benson
16(1713)Lets Pretend
17(1714)Childrens Hour
17(1715)Joe Penner
18(1716)Bobbie Benson
19(1717)Lady Next Door
19(1718)Bobbie Benson

1935 Mar.
19(----)Audition
20(1719)Bobbie Benson
20(1720)Amer.School Air
21(1721)Bobbie Benson
21(1722)Show Boat
22(1723)Bobbie Benson
23(1724)Lets Pretend
23(1725)Lady Next Door
24(1726)Childrens Hour
24(1727)Man.Merry Go.Rd.
25(1728)Bobbie Benson
26(1729)Lady Next Door
26(1730)Records
27(1731)Amer.School Air
28(1732)Show Boat
30(1733)Lets Pretend
30(1734)Ldy.Next Door
31(1735)Childrens Hour
31(1736)Lux
31(1737)Man,Merry Go.Rd.
Apr.
1(1738)Records
x1(1739)Bobbie Benson
2(1740)Records
2(1741)Bobbie Benson
v2(1742)Lady Next Door
3(1743)Amer.School Of Air

The little black notebook of radio credits, kept by Frederick Tetzloff.

CHAPTER 1

German-born Frederick Edward Tetzloff crossed the Atlantic as a young man. Upon arrival in the New York harbor, his only possessions were a well-worn valise containing a few changes of clothing, a faded photograph of his family back home, three books, and a little tin box that held his razor, a comb, brush, two bars of homemade soap, a wooden spool of black thread, some needles and pins, a few spare buttons, and a small pair of sharp scissors. In the pocket of his tattered jacket he had a notebook and some pencils, and concealed deep in his vest pocket was his coin purse containing his entire fortune—a few bills, neatly folded.

The immigrant took a dingy room in a cheap boarding house, the rent also including sparse meals. Very sparse meals. The room was small and stuffy and the only furnishings were a narrow cot with a hard, flat mattress stuffed with straw, and a three-legged chair propped up in the corner, against the wall. There were no windows and the only light came from a bare light bulb dangling from a frayed wire from the water-stained ceiling.

Tetzloff's American beginnings were indeed humble, but he had a keen mind, eager to learn. Despite the language barrier Fredrick lost no time in finding himself a job sweeping floors and emptying the rubbish barrel in a small cluttered German grocery store. Sometimes, after a busy day, the owner would give him some day-old bread or buns, and a slice of hard cheese. The immigrant kept his eyes and ears open, and closely observed his new surroundings. Slowly he began to learn the new language. In doing so, he also learned some peculiar phrases, such as "Hey you," "Sez who?" and "Get lost."

Back in his room he read his books, and kept his hair trimmed with his scissors. When he noticed the many newspapers that were left discarded on streetcar seats, he would pick them up and take them back to his room and study them carefully. Even if the newsprint was in Hebrew or Chinese, he pondered over them.

As his command of English improved he was able to move on to better paying jobs. After landing a job in a clothing factory he was able to rent a furnished one-room apartment on the top floor of a brownstone tenement. He had seven flights of stairs to climb to reach his new quarters, but he didn't mind. He walked with a quick step, holding his shoulders erect, and his clear blue eyes focused straight ahead. He kept his trousers pressed and a fresh shine on his only pair of shoes. He practiced reading aloud from his books and newspapers. Eventually he gained the courage to join in conversations with his co-workers, who quickly shortened his name to "Fred." He was personable, and formed friendships easily, as he cheerfully looked forward to a better way of life in America.

Red-haired Jessie Campbell was born in Glasgow and was also a recent immigrant to America. Her devoted family back in Scotland had little need to worry about their daughter being alone in the big wicked city. The lass was totally self-reliant and had a definite air of determination about her. Miss Campbell was one Scottish lassie who had matters well in hand. Having traced her ancestry back through many generations, she was proud to boast that she shared kinship not only to the Duke of Argyle, but on through to no less than William the Conqueror. She dressed well, but conservatively, and was the kind of vibrant young woman who did not have to wear a bright plaid coat, nor a large hat with a high plume on it, to stand out in a crowd, not even in New York City.

Jessie Campbell Tetley was always proud of her Scottish ancestry.

As a girl back in Scotland, her favorite music hall entertainer had always been the legendary Harry Lauder. She frugally saved her pennies to buy his phonograph records and played them over and over, memorizing the lyrics. The girl remembered every story and anecdote she had ever heard or read about him. It was well known that the famed entertainer had a very feisty temperament. An oft-told tale concerned his appearance before a vast crowd. Someone in the audience stood up and called out, "Louder! We canna hear ye!" Lauder shouted right back, "I am nay gonna strain ma voice. If ye are deaf in the ears, it nay be ma fault. I am an actor and a singer. I am nay a roarer, and I did nay come here to roar, and I am nay gonna roar. If ye canna hear me it is because ye are nay listenin' good enough. If ye are a sittin' way back in the cheap seats—pay a few more pennies an' buy a better seat—up front!" Despite his effrontery Lauder was beloved by all.

Born in Portobello, Scotland on August 4, 1870, as a lad he began to work in the mines. To escape such a fate, he started to perform in amateur shows, and kept at it. Before he reached the age of 30 he had become a star and appeared on the London stage, singing his famous tunes such as "The Lass of Killiecrankie," "Roaming in the Gloamin'," "A Wee Deoch an' Doris," "Auld Lang Syne," and "I Love a Lassie."

Lauder began making records in 1902, and within two years 50 of his songs had been preserved on wax. He recorded for such well-known labels as Pathé, Edison, Zonophone, and Victor. One of the last songs he ever recorded, and on which he delightfully rolled his r's, was "Always Take Care of Your Pennies."

Lauder did not have a particularly good or clear singing voice but audiences loved to listen to his songs, stories and jokes. He had an appeal to all nationalities. His arrival in any town or city was always hailed with a parade of Scottish pipers down the main street.

During World War I Lauder was the first major star to volunteer his services to entertain the Allied troops. His son was a Captain in the Army and lost his life in battle. In recognition of his valiant efforts, he was knighted and became Sir Harry Lauder in 1918. He died in his 80th year on February 26, 1950. During his final years Lauder made repeated "farewell tours," both here and abroad.

Immigrants Fred Tetzloff and Jessie Campbell traveled from far away lands to meet on an island that had been sold by the Indians for a much-quoted bargain price of $24. To be sure, they were an odd match, but it was a combination that worked well.

One of the first things that Fred noticed about Jessie when he first laid eyes on her was not only her burnished tresses, but her very apparent self-assurance. After meeting by chance on a few occasions, Fred invited her out to dinner. He ordered weinerschnitzel for two. When he asked her how she liked it, she smiled and said, "Bonnie." Secretly she would have preferred roast leg of lamb with mint jelly. On their way back downtown she took him to a small Scottish bakery and introduced him to scones. They began to see each other more often. They went out to Coney Island and rode on the gigantic Ferris wheel, and ate hot dogs and cotton candy.

Fred was hired as a U.S. postal worker and proposed marriage to Jessie. She accepted without hesitation and they were wed and settled in a modest apartment. He was now earning a comfortable living and she frugally managed the household finances. Life went well and the couple was blessed by the birth of a son they named Albert. He was an amiable child with his father's cheerful ways. He kept his mother busy chasing after him.

When the boy was old enough to toddle around the apartment his mother tried to sit him down long enough to listen to some of her favorite Lauder records, in hopes he would memorize the words. Her hope was in vain. Albert had no interest in doing any such thing, and he would wail and ask to be carried downstairs where he could sit on the front stoop with the other tenement children. Reluctantly, Jessie complied.

Albert was pampered until a second son arrived on June 2, 1915. He was named Walter, and almost from the time he appeared on the scene, there seemed to be something very special about him. He was of average size and weight, with sandy colored hair and clear blue eyes.

Walter at 1 year and 4 months old.

Curious neighbors came from far and near for a preview peek at the adorable new infant. All agreed that there was definitely something "special" about Walter Tetzloff. Just what it was, no one knew for certain, at the time—but time would tell. He did not glow in the dark, or float from his cradle near the ceiling, nor was there a visible halo around his cherubic head. There was, however, a special sparkle in the way he smiled at everyone, and a definite firmness in the way his chubby little hand gripped his father's finger, and a gentle tenderness in the way he lovingly snuggled against his mother's breast. It would have come as no surprise that he would at any moment stand and take a bow.

It didn't take long for his mother to begin to recognize her wee son's great potential to become a professional entertainer, just like her lifelong idol. She placed his cradle near the phonograph and began to play her favorite recordings, over and over. The babe gurgled with glee and turned his wee ear towards the sound of the music and began to kick his chubby little legs, in what Jessie imagined, was in perfect rhythm with the lilting tunes. She nearly jumped for joy and her spirits soared higher than a kite on a Scottish hillside. At long last—her dream was coming true. Every time she changed a diaper she carried a new stack of records to the machine and cranked it up, and one by one she played them for her attentive son. To further encourage him, she wrapped a plaid scarf around his wee shoulders.

By the time Walter had reached the age of 3 he had memorized the words and could sing along. She was in Scottish heaven hearing her bonnie wee laddie singing her favorite songs. Next his mother began to teach him Lauder's gestures and mannerisms. When she placed a tam-o-shanter on his wee head she made certain it was tilted at the right angle so that the tassel did not dangle in his face.

Fred's work with the postal department brought about a family move to the town of Ridgefield, New Jersey where they rented a house at 128 Edwin Street. Also making her home with them was Jessie's unmarried sister, Anna Campbell.

Jessie was a good cook and neat housekeeper, but she did nay go in for any frills. All furnishings had to be serviceable and durable. Her only wee bit of frivolity was some bright Tartan plaid curtains and pillows.

Supper was served promptly when Fred returned home from the post office. A typical evening meal was a steaming bowl of "Scotch broth" that Jessie had simmered for long hours in a black iron kettle, along with some freshly baked scones, hot from the oven. She followed her mother's recipe to make the broth from mutton, barley, and bits of carrots, turnips, celery and onion. The meal was often topped off with a big slice of warm gingerbread with lemon sauce.

At the age of five Walter was bundled off to kindergarten at Lincoln School, where his teachers were very impressed with his many abilities, for one so young. When he began to entertain the other children with his Scottish songs, it became quite evident that the boy had been taught a great deal at home. If a visitor came into the classroom, the teacher would call upon her star pupil to entertain. Wee Walter had mastered an authentic Highland accent and could turn it off and on at will. At home he entertained the family, as well as the neighbors.

In the new neighborhood, Jessie's Scottish pride and stubbornness often got her in trouble. She carried herself with rigid regality and patrician dignity, which others often mistook for haughtiness, or sheer arrogance. She was outspoken and quick to fly off the handle, and there was many a skirmish with the neighbors. She was not one to spoil her children and was a strict disciplinarian, but she also possessed warm maternal instincts, both emotional and impulsive. At times, for no apparent reason, she would throw her strong arms around her sons and clasp them to her ample bosom. She reared her sons to be gentlemen. They were always obedient, polite and respectful to their elders.

Young Walter in one of his first photos in costume.

Meanwhile, Walter continued to learn more Scottish songs and his mother also taught him some of Sir Harry's monologues and recitations.

The boy's first important public performance was at a meeting of The Daughters of Scotia, one of the several organizations of which Jessie was a member. For the occasion she made him a wee kilt, and to round out the effect, she rented a set of miniature bagpipes. To be sure, he was a sensation—and "wowed 'em."

Being an active member of a number of church and civic clubs, Jessie was always among the first to volunteer to serve on the entertainment committee for any fund-raising event. She took full advantage of every possible opportunity to give her talented son a chance to perform before an audience.

And so it came to pass that Walter received frequent calls for his special services. His mother realized that there was more than a good chance for him to become a professional entertainer. Now was the time to come up with a more professional sounding name for him, especially one that also sounded more Scottish. Every one of their acquaintances joined in the fun. It was Jessie who came up with the idea of borrowing from the brand name of her favorite tea.

A vintage, unusual photo of young Tetley not in Scottish costume. Early 1930's.

Back in England in 1856 the Tetley brothers, Joseph and Edward established a tea merchant business in London. The brothers soon began to disagree, and parted company. Joseph took on a new partner, Joseph Ackland. Years later, it was his son Joseph Tetley, Jr. who took over the business and brought the name to great prominence. In 1888 their product was distributed in America, and in 1913 "Tetley Tea" was an internationally known name. In America in 1920, after much experimentation, the tea company introduced the novel idea of producing a small packet of tea that could be placed in a single cup or pot, for quick and easy brewing. One of the major obstacles in making the idea practical was the creation of a special tissue for the bag, so that it did not taint the color or taste of the tea. The "tea bag" became a way of life in America in 1939, but did not become popular in England until years later.

Both parents agreed that "Walter Tetley" would be a good choice. Then, as an afterthought, Jessie thought that placing the name "Campbell" in the middle would make it sound even more Scottish.

At the age of seven "Walter Campbell Tetley," accompanied by his

Walter Tetley, early 1930's.

mother, set out on a vaudeville tour for the Keith Orpheum circuit. They toured throughout the East Coast, granting him an excellent opportunity to develop his Wee Sir Harry Lauder act more fully.

Jessie quickly became the epitome of flamboyant stage mothers. She had a very persuasive nature and could drive a hard bargain, and knew exactly how to deal with tight-fisted booking agents. They could readily see from the no-nonsense hats she wore and the size of the pocketbook she carried, as well as the firm stare behind her wire-rimmed glasses, that she possessed a very keen business sense. She had a pertinacity that was more than obvious. As she sized up the business office, anyone could guess that her favorite key on the typewriter was the "$".

Mrs. Tetley left no stone unturned in paving the path for the road to success for her son. She mastered her own "bargaining technique" that was practically foolproof. During a bargain session, at the most effective point, she would pause and remove her spectacles. Then, with very dramatic gestures she would unfasten the clasp on her pocketbook with a very loud snap. Slowly she would reach deep to the bottom and extract an immaculately white, lace-edged handkerchief, and very methodically begin to wipe the lenses of her glasses, taking her own good-natured time to do so. All the while, the wheels of her calculating mind would be spinning. She would try to envision the size of the auditorium, the exact number of seats, both balcony and orchestra, and the price of admission to be charged. She would add on percentages, traveling expenses, as well as cleaning bills. She would tally up all of the figures in her mind. When a sum had been reached, she carefully refolded the handkerchief into a perfect triangle, and slowly replaced it inside her pocketbook. For effect, she would refasten the clasp with a very dramatic *SNAP*!

When, at last, she finally announced the figure she had reached "for Walter's services," all agents knew beyond the shadow of a doubt that

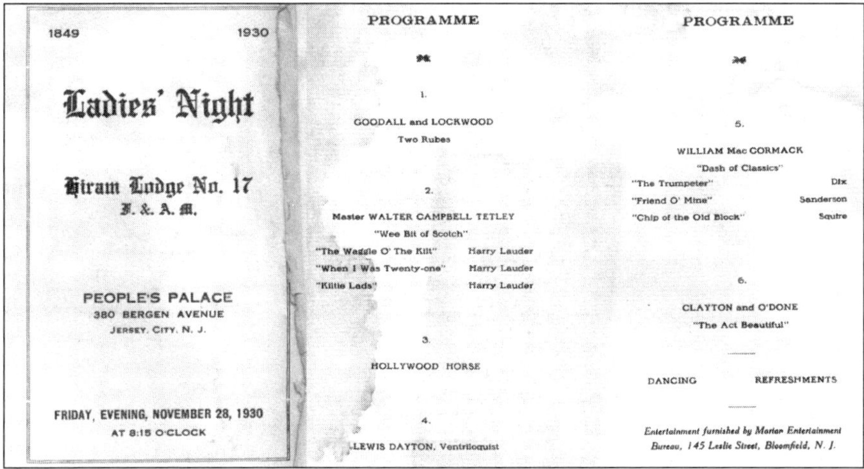

1849 1930

Ladies' Night

Hiram Lodge No. 17
F. & A. M.

PEOPLE'S PALACE
380 BERGEN AVENUE
JERSEY CITY, N. J.

FRIDAY, EVENING, NOVEMBER 28, 1930
AT 8:15 O'CLOCK

PROGRAMME

1.
GOODALL and LOCKWOOD
Two Rubes

2.
Master WALTER CAMPBELL TETLEY
"Wee Bit of Scotch"

"The Waggle O' The Kilt"	Harry Lauder
"When I Was Twenty-one"	Harry Lauder
"Kiltie Lads"	Harry Lauder

3.
HOLLYWOOD HORSE

4.
LEWIS DAYTON, Ventriloquist

PROGRAMME

5.
WILLIAM Mac CORMACK
"Dash of Classics"

"The Trumpeter"	Dix
"Friend O' Mine"	Sanderson
"Chip of the Old Block"	Squire

6.
CLAYTON and O'DONE
"The Act Beautiful"

DANCING REFRESHMENTS

Entertainment furnished by Marian Entertainment Bureau, 145 Leslie Street, Bloomfield, N. J.

there was absolutely nothing in the world that could possibly change her mind, not in the least bit. They all gave in.

Backstage, Jessie was her most majestic best. The most stout-hearted of stage managers would quake in their boots when they saw her standing in the wings. She would waggle her gloved finger at the poor soul who was waiting to close the curtain, and indicate that she was watching, and he better not close the main drape whilst her son was still onstage. She would also signal the lighting man to keep the main spotlight focused on "the star of the show." And woe be to any slow-moving stagehand that did not clear the scenery fast enough to suit her; she would merely shove them aside and do it herself. If it had not been for Walter's enormous talents and his very amiable personality, and sure-fire ability to "wow"

Walter Tetley, center stage, in 1928.

Madge "The Lady Next Door" Tucker seated behind the figure of Krazy Kat, surrounded by many of the young actors she discovered. Walter is standing at far right, in pirate costume and false sideburns and mustache. Early 1930's.

WALTER CAMPBELL TETLEY
"The Wee Sir Harry Lauder"

Under the management of Frances Rockefeller King. Private Entertainment Department of the National Broadcasting Company.

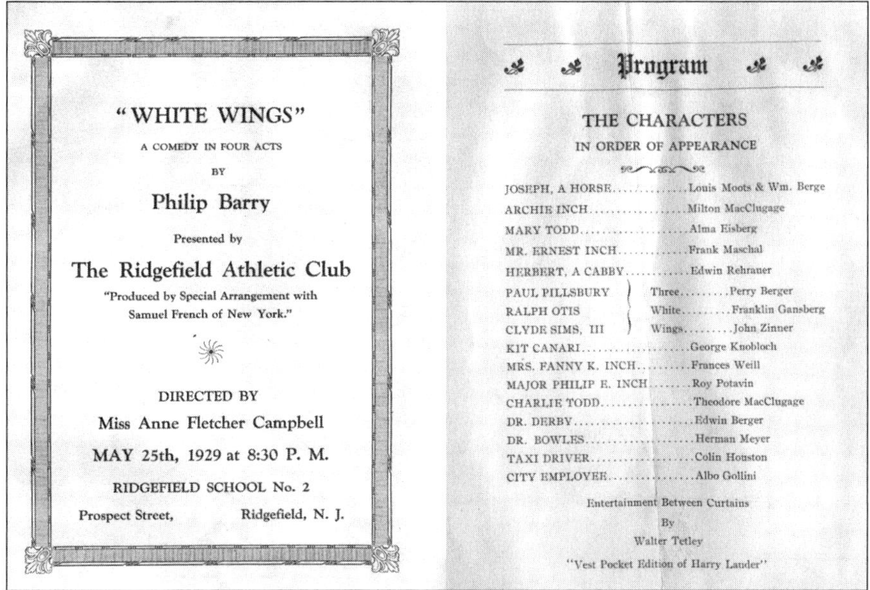

"WHITE WINGS"

A COMEDY IN FOUR ACTS

BY

Philip Barry

Presented by

The Ridgefield Athletic Club

"Produced by Special Arrangement with Samuel French of New York."

DIRECTED BY

Miss Anne Fletcher Campbell

MAY 25th, 1929 at 8:30 P. M.

RIDGEFIELD SCHOOL No. 2

Prospect Street, Ridgefield, N. J.

Program

THE CHARACTERS

IN ORDER OF APPEARANCE

JOSEPH, A HORSE............Louis Moots & Wm. Berge
ARCHIE INCH................Milton MacClugage
MARY TODD...................Alma Eisberg
MR. ERNEST INCH.............Frank Maschal
HERBERT, A CABBY............Edwin Rehrauer
PAUL PILLSBURY — Three........Perry Berger
RALPH OTIS — White........Franklin Gansberg
CLYDE SIMS, III — Wings........John Zinner
KIT CANARI..................George Knobloch
MRS. FANNY K. INCH..........Frances Weill
MAJOR PHILIP E. INCH........Roy Potavin
CHARLIE TODD................Theodore MacClugage
DR. DERBY...................Edwin Berger
DR. BOWLES..................Herman Meyer
TAXI DRIVER.................Colin Houston
CITY EMPLOYEE...............Albo Gollini

Entertainment Between Curtains

By

Walter Tetley

"Vest Pocket Edition of Harry Lauder"

any audience, they probably would have been barred from entering the theater. As it turned out, he was often held over or booked for another engagement.

The tour behind them, the Tetleys returned home to Ridgefield. Another of the lad's important engagements back home took place at the People's Palace in Jersey City for a special "Ladies Night" appearance at one of his mother's Lodges. For the occasion he was billed as "Master Walter Tetley—A Wee Bit of Scotland."

Stars of The Lady Next Door, *Audrey Egan and Walter Tetley, share a soda in the early 1930's.*

Walter had always been a small child for his age, so it was appropriate to adopt "Wee" as part of his professional name. It was during the tour that Jessie first became aware that her son was much shorter than other children. Walter's size had not increased due to a

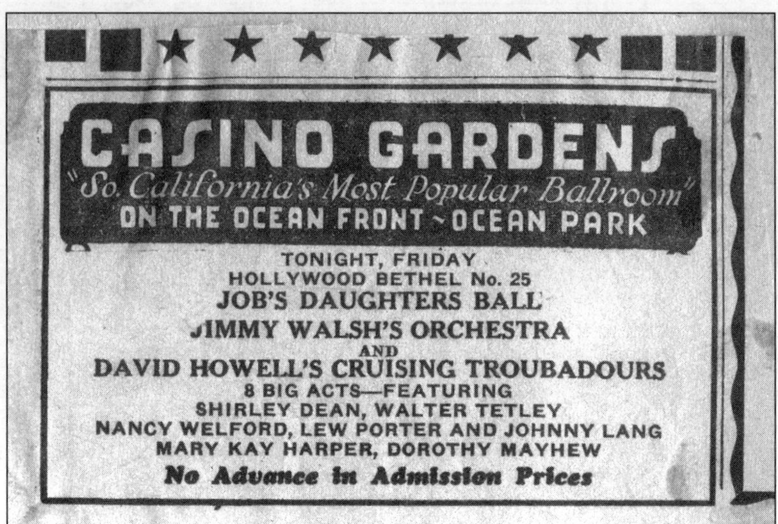

malfunction of his thyroid gland. The condition was caused by an imbalance of Thyroxin, a hormone that regulates growth. If a reliable physician had been consulted about the problem, it was not recorded in the family papers. His size was a DARK secret to be kept and used to its fullest advantage for his career as a child performer. As he grew in age, his mother cut his age in half for promotional reasons, insisting that the adolescent was still a child. "Wee Sir Harry Lauder" lived on in bookings.

In November of 1928 Walter's abundant talents received recognition in the pages of the *New York Times* when he appeared in the youthful cast of an unknown revue. The 13-year-old was decked out in full Scottish garb, seated center stage.

It might be assumed that his Aunt Anna Campbell was a teacher at Ridgefield High School, for on May 25, 1929 she directed the Senior Class play, *White Wings*, a four-act comedy by Philip Barry. She arranged to have her talented nephew, "The Vest Pocket Edition of Sir Harry Lauder," entertain between acts while the scenery was being changed. The audience responded with a standing ovation.

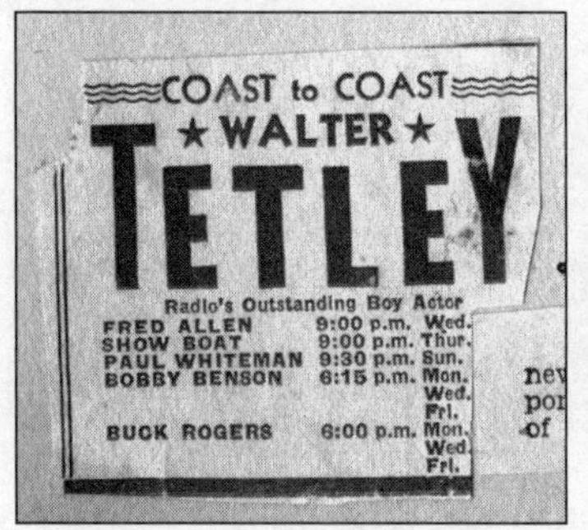

Ambitious Jessie began to envision new horizons for her son to conquer. But… what? A family friend solved the dilemma by suggesting that the talented boy be taken to NBC's broadcasting studios in New York City to audition for RADIO. The agent-mother lost no time. On Saturday, February 8, 1930 Walter auditioned for NBC's *The Children's Hour* variety program. He passed the audition with flying colors and was signed to sing and give his Lauder impersonation on the program the following day. Once again he created a sensation, and his radio career was off and running.

On the strength of his radio debut performance he was invited by children's radio programming pioneer Madge Tucker to appear on her Saturday afternoon broadcasts of *The Barn Show*. She auditioned talented youngsters and coached them to take part in weekly dramatized stories that she also wrote. Miss Tucker had been cited as "The Maker of Stars." One network observed, "In her hands, to a great extent, rests the future of radio. The youngsters she trains are the celebrities of the next generation, who by virtue of their early microphone education, will be able to take care of the eventual requirements of broadcasting."

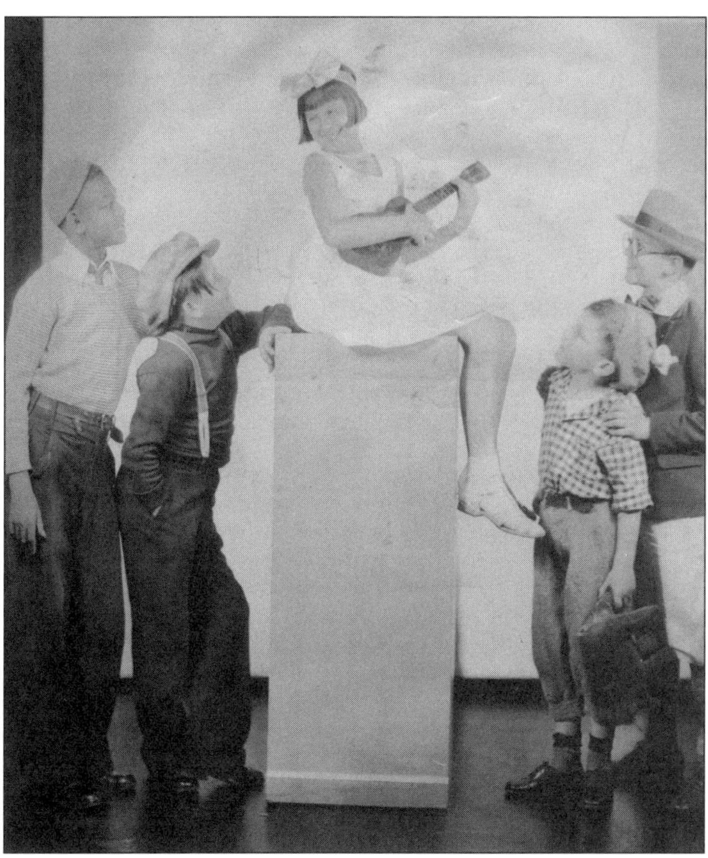

Walter and kids in an unknown review, early 1930's.

Madge Tucker recognized Walter's abundant talent and encouraged him to become, in addition to being an extraordinary impersonator and singer, a dramatic actor as well.

She was also known to young listeners as *The Lady Next Door* who inspired neighboring kids to put on a show in her barn. As early as 1929 she had begun a 15-minute sustaining series on NBC. Her young acting proteges were known as "The Magic Circle" and aired dramatized stories. Among the many recognizable names on the long list of her troupe were: Florence and Billy Halop, Nancy Kelly, Bob Hastings, Rosalyn Silber, Jimmy McCallion, Audrey Egan, Jackie Kelk, plus many more—and soon to be added—Walter Tetley.

Another of her regular broadcasts was known as *Coast to Coast on a Bus*. The hour-long variety program was filled with variety acts and leaned heavily towards dramatic sketches. Walter, being adept at many different dialects, had many opportunities to emote.

The host of the show was Milton J. Cross who also served as the "conductor" of the big white bus that traveled cross-country, making stops

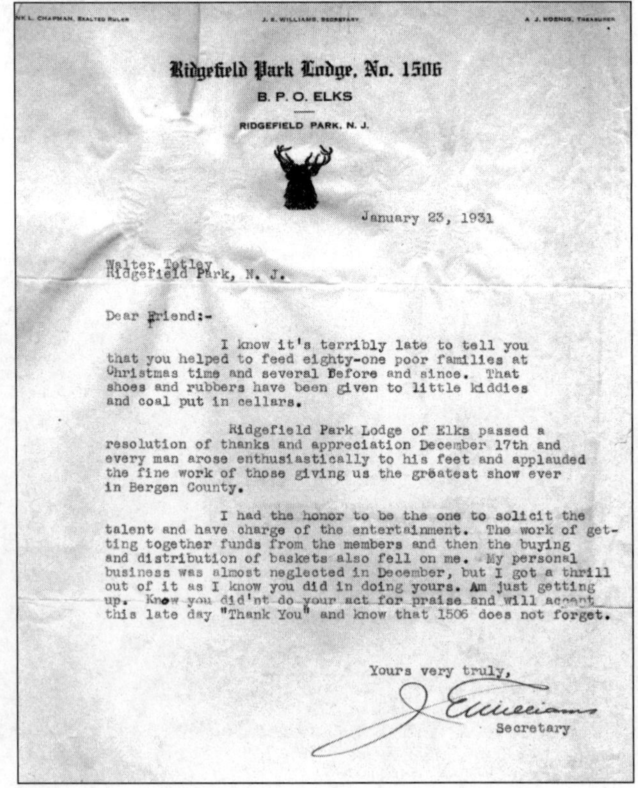

...K L. CHAPMAN, EXALTED RULER　　J. E. WILLIAMS, SECRETARY　　A. J. KOENIG, TREASURER

Ridgefield Park Lodge, No. 1506
B. P. O. ELKS
RIDGEFIELD PARK, N. J.

January 23, 1931

Walter Tetley
Ridgefield Park, N. J.

Dear Friend:-

I know it's terribly late to tell you that you helped to feed eighty-one poor families at Christmas time and several before and since. That shoes and rubbers have been given to little kiddies and coal put in cellars.

Ridgefield Park Lodge of Elks passed a resolution of thanks and appreciation December 17th and every man arose enthusiastically to his feet and applauded the fine work of those giving us the grëatest show ever in Bergen County.

I had the honor to be the one to solicit the talent and have charge of the entertainment. The work of getting together funds from the members and then the buying and distribution of baskets also fell on me. My personal business was almost neglected in December, but I got a thrill out of it as I know you did in doing yours. Am just getting up. Know you did'nt do your act for praise and will accept this late day "Thank You" and know that 1506 does not forget.

Yours very truly,

J. E. Williams
Secretary

along the way. He would then park the bus, honk the horn, and introduce the next act or sketch. Cross was a very familiar voice to listeners since 1922 when he first became an announcer for NBC. In 1931 he gained a vast following by taking over as the host/commentator on the weekly Saturday afternoon broadcasts from the stage of the Metropolitan Opera House.

Walter began his long association with Madge Tucker on the Saturday afternoon broadcast of February 15, 1930, and remained a steady fixture through August of 1937, shortly before he ventured off to Hollywood.

With the responsibility of a heavy weekly broadcasting schedule to maintain, Walter was fortunate that he had full family support behind him. Everyone's personal schedule was altered to comply with his. In addition to all of the broadcasting duties he had to fulfill, his mother also saw to it that there were plenty of personal appearances to make.

On December 17, 1930 he joined several other acts to give a benefit sponsored by the Elks Lodge No. 1507 of Ridgefield Park. In recognition of his participation, a month later he received a letter of appreciation from the event's coordinator, which began:

"I know it is terribly late to tell you that you helped feel 81 poor families at Christmas time, and several more, since and before. Shoes and boots have been given to little kiddies, and coal put in cellars."

The social responsibility that he felt never left him, and he always tried to do as much as he possibly could, with the talent that had been given him.

Despite his spreading fame and accumulating fortune Tetley remained unspoiled and unassuming. He always tried to avoid looking conspicuous. Other than an inexpensive wristwatch that his parents had given him, the only jewelry he wore was a ring that had been given to him by a relative who had been killed in World War I. The plain ring remained dented where a bullet had struck it.

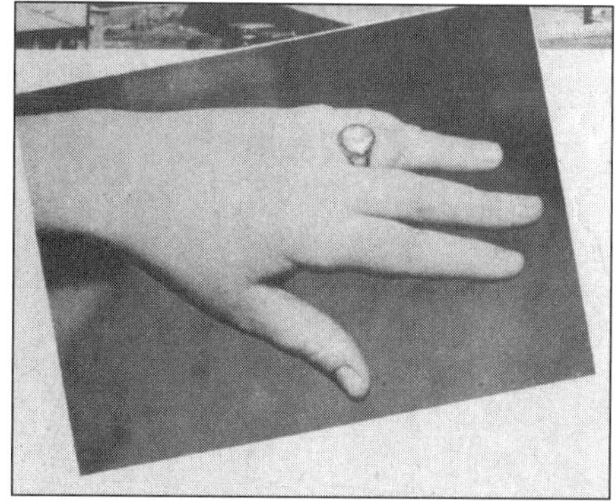

Gift from a relative.

Chapter 2

Less than a year after his radio debut Walter was at NBC studios on February 3, 1931 when a child actor failed to appear for a new program that was about to go on the air. The frantic director, Raymond Knight saw Walter getting off an elevator. He knew the young actor's capabilities and had every confidence in him. Knight snatched him off the elevator, and with less than five minutes before air time, a script was pressed into his hands and he was ushered up to the microphone. All he was told was that he was to read the role of "Bobby Lee," the smart-alecky brat son of young parents. Without the benefit of rehearsal he gave a sparkling performance, and as a result he was signed to play the role in the quarter-hour broadcasts of *Raising Junior*, six times each week. The program told of the woes of the harassed young parents of two sons, bratty Bobby, and his younger sibling, called "Junior." The parents were played by a real life married couple.

Throughout the early 1930's Tetley's radio appearances racked up at an incredible rate, sometimes as many as five different shows a day. The little black notebook recorded shows such as *Uncle Abe & David*, a quarter-hour series starring Parker Fennelly and Arthur Allen; *The Coo Coo Hour*, actually *The Cuckoo Hour*, a quarter-hour variety show; and *Eno*, really *The Eno Crime Club*, "another action-packed radio riddle—giving you a chance to play detective yourself. Listen carefully so you can solve the puzzle from the clues in tonight's episode." This series, presented in both quarter and half-hour formats featured the main character "Spencer Dean," a famous private eye known as "The Manhunter."

Other series included: *Emerald Isle*, a children's adventure series; *Big*

"Wee Sir Harry Lauder"

Time Radio Household (noted in the black notebook as simply *Household*), a variety show on which Walter presented his Wee Sir Harry Lauder impersonation; *Friendship Town*, a variety series on WJZ; and *The Adventures of Helen & Mary*, presenting children's stories, predating *Let's Pretend*. Along with all these new shows Walter kept busy with his regular series, and enough auditions to prove his demand was high. More often than not, a day or two after an audition, Walter would find himself on a new series.

He performed his "Wee Sir Harry" act many times on radio, gaining enough media attention to herald several glowing reviews. Entertaining at the Junior Mechanics' Dinner in Lackawanna, Pennsylvania Walter "took the audience and thousands of listeners by storm. This young lad, twelve years of age, gave imitations of Harry Lauder in songs and sayings that kept his hearers in hearty laughter. His pleasing personality, with a smile that can't wear off, and his various gestures mystified the audience and left an impression that will long be remembered."

Local political and civic leaders who attended the tribute to America's two outstanding statesmen at the Washington-Lincoln banquet in the Hotel Jermyn were equally impressed with the live act.

With the accompaniment of

Greetings

The Rotary Club of Yonkers extends a cordial welcome to its friends in appreciation of the support given this presentation of their Fourth Annual Minstrel.

The entertainment represents our sincere endeavor to make the evening an enjoyable one for you and also helps us to raise the funds for our Boys' Work. Your patronage insures the success of the Boys' Work Committee in financing our summer camp activities for the underprivileged boys of this city.

The measure of your pleasure bespeaks our success.

ROTARY THANKS YOU

—o—

Program

OVERTURE—*"Faust"* - - - - Craven's Orchestra
OPENING CHORUS - - - - - Entire Company
SOLO—*"Ah, Sweet Mystery of Life"* - - Werner G. Klebe
END SONG—*"You're Driving Me Crazy"* - Arthur Witte
SPECIALTY - - - - - - Walter Tetley
END SONG—*"It Takes a Long, Tall Brown Skin Gal"* Ed Spitz
SAXOPHONE SOLO - - - - - Alvin Weisfeldt
SPECIALTY - - - - - - - Sally Wilson
END SONG—*"Hello Beautiful"* - - - Harold Garrity
SONG AND DANCE SPECIALTY - Thelma Hassett's Pupils
SOLO—*"Friend of Mine"* - - - Norman Jolliffe
END SONG—*"Ninety-nine Out of a Hundred"* Jud McCarthy
CLOSING CHORUS - - - - - Entire Company

—o—

Grateful acknowledgement is made to Thelma Hassett for the Girl Dancing Specialty; Harry Daniels for Lithographs.

WALTER TETLEY

OVER 2000 BROADCASTS
ON 150 DIFFERENT PROGRAMS

Available For

Radio - Stage - Screen
Recording - Concert

WORLD - TELEGRAM

SATURDAY, APRIL 13th, 1935.

A FEW GET FOOTHOLD.

Walter Tetley, a remarkably talented boy comedian who appears occasionally with Fred Allen, started out on that Sunday morning WJZ kids' show.

ALBANY EVENING NEWS

ALBANY, N. Y., APRIL 22, 1935

Miss Malone says:

"I would like permission to toss a bouquet in the general direction of Walter Tetley, brilliant 14-year-old radio star.

"Of course you have heard Walter playing the part of Waldo, a tough kid, on Fred Allen's program. You may also have heard him on 'Let's Pretend,' Columbia's Saturday morning offering. It is possible you may have detected his voice on other presentations during the week, sometimes in the advertising skits. A very busy young man, is Walter.

"His impersonation of a Scotch youngster on a recent Allen broadcast was magnificent. The burr was not overdone, as is generally the case. Indeed, all of this lad's efforts, so far as I'm concerned, are quite satisfactory. I think he ranks right up there with the best of the best, and it is with sincerity that I say: "You're the tops, Walter; you're the tops."

THE ONE DIALER

Master Walter Tetley, one of the cleverest youngsters on the air, did a great job Monday evening. Portraying a bright-as-steel young Scotch lad during the CBS Bobby Benson show, Walter and a young miss who played opposite him, stole the show from the adult members of the cast.

RADIOLAND

MAY, 1935

Perhaps the most promising comedian of the future is a fourteen-year-old lad—Walter Tetley of *Buck Rogers* and *Bar X Days* fame, who has been a featured radio player for eight years. Walter is amazingly mature and workmanlike, switching from character to character with the ease and deftness of a Ted Bergman. Watching him in a rehearsal of the Fred Allen show, of which cast he is a regular member, it was surprising to see him portray five different characters in three different dialects in the space of a half hour.

From the Allen rehearsal he rushed to an adjoining studio where Miss Tucker was putting her kids through their paces for the Sunday morning Children's Hour. She requested Walter to sing one of the songs he had brought back from Europe after an extensive tour through the British Isles, preferably one with patter in some dialect to serve as a setting for the number. Walter replied casually: "I haven't one with patter, but I can write some in." And write some in he did right there in the control room. Many a highly-paid comedian tearing his hair for new ideas and gags would have been proud to admit ownership to the Cockney monologue this fourteen-year-old prodigy dashed off so glibly.

For Booking Information, Apply Sam Ross, N.B.C. Artists Service, or Walter Tetley, 5 Beverly

THE ROTARY CLUB

OF YONKERS

Samuel Hayward, *President*

FOURTH ANNUAL
MINSTREL SHOW

WEDNESDAY EVENING, MARCH 11, 1931
Eight-Fifteen O'Clock
Nathaniel Hawthorne Junior High School

Greetings

The Rotary Club of Yonkers extends a cordial welcome to its friends in appreciation of the support given this presentation of their Fourth Annual Minstrel.

The entertainment represents our sincere endeavor to make the evening an enjoyable one for you and also helps us to raise the funds for our Boys' Work. Your patronage insures the success of the Boys' Work Committee in financing our summer camp activities for the underprivileged boys of this city.

The measure of your pleasure bespeaks our success.

ROTARY THANKS YOU

—o—

Program

Overture—*"Faust"* - - - - - Craven's Orchestra
Opening Chorus - - - - - - Entire Company
Solo—*"Ah, Sweet Mystery of Life"* - - Werner G. Klebe
End Song—*"You're Driving Me Crazy"* - Arthur Witte
Specialty - - - - - - - Walter Tetley
End Song—*"It Takes a Long, Tall Brown Skin Gal"* Ed Spitz
Saxophone Solo - - - - - - Alvin Weisfeldt
Specialty - - - - - - - - Sally Wilson
End Song—*"Hello Beautiful"* - - - Harold Garrity
Song and Dance Specialty - Thelma Hassett's Pupils
Solo—*"Friend of Mine"* - - - Norman Jolliffe
End Song—*"Ninety-nine Out of a Hundred"* Jud McCarthy
Closing Chorus - - - - - Entire Company

—o—

Grateful acknowledgement is made to Thelma Hassett for the Girl Dancing Specialty; Harry Daniels for Lithographs.

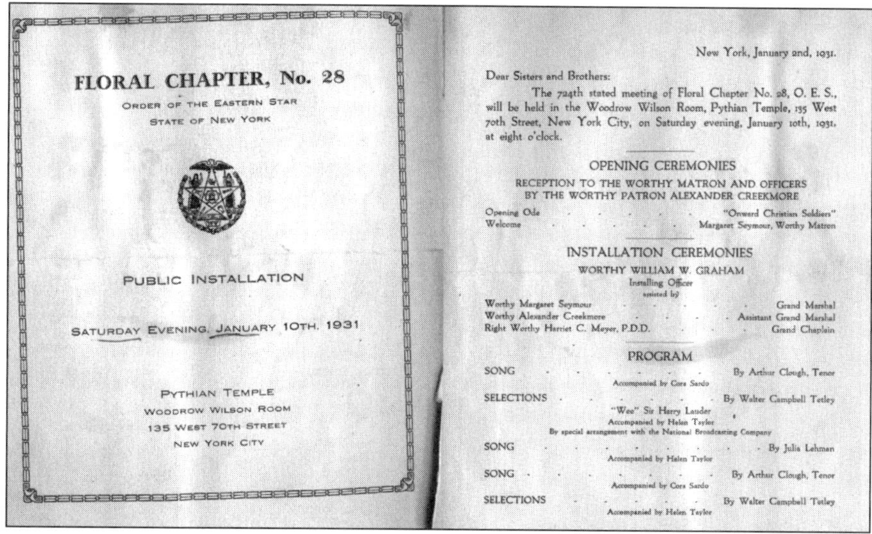

FLORAL CHAPTER, No. 28

ORDER OF THE EASTERN STAR

STATE OF NEW YORK

PUBLIC INSTALLATION

SATURDAY EVENING, JANUARY 10TH, 1931

PYTHIAN TEMPLE

WOODROW WILSON ROOM

135 WEST 70TH STREET

NEW YORK CITY

New York, January 2nd, 1931.

Dear Sisters and Brothers:

The 724th stated meeting of Floral Chapter No. 28, O. E. S., will be held in the Woodrow Wilson Room, Pythian Temple, 135 West 70th Street, New York City, on Saturday evening, January 10th, 1931, at eight o'clock.

OPENING CEREMONIES

RECEPTION TO THE WORTHY MATRON AND OFFICERS BY THE WORTHY PATRON ALEXANDER CREEKMORE

Opening Ode . . . . "Onward Christian Soldiers"
Welcome . . . . Margaret Seymour, Worthy Matron

INSTALLATION CEREMONIES

WORTHY WILLIAM W. GRAHAM
Installing Officer
assisted by

Worthy Margaret Seymour . . . . Grand Marshal
Worthy Alexander Creekmore . . . . . Assistant Grand Marshal
Right Worthy Harriet C. Meyer, P.D.D. . . . . Grand Chaplain

PROGRAM

SONG . . . . By Arthur Clough, Tenor
Accompanied by Cora Sardo

SELECTIONS . . . . By Walter Campbell Tetley
"Wee" Sir Harry Lauder
Accompanied by Helen Taylor
By special arrangement with the National Broadcasting Company

SONG . . . . By Julia Lehman
Accompanied by Helen Taylor

SONG . . . . By Arthur Clough, Tenor
Accompanied by Cora Sardo

SELECTIONS . . . . By Walter Campbell Tetley
Accompanied by Helen Taylor

Helen Taylor at the piano, Walter performed his wee songs for the benefit of the 28th Floral Chapter of the Order of the Eastern Star at Pythian Temple on 135 West 70th Street in New York City on January 10, 1931.

Wee Walter did his "specialty act" for the Rotary Club of Yonkers' fourth annual Minstrel Show on Wednesday evening, March 11, 1931. The completely musical night took place at the Nathaniel Hawthorne Junior High School.

Tetley may have been becoming a national radio star, but his mother realized the significance of public performances, and giving something back to the community. That moral sense was obviously highly ingrained in Walter at an early age.

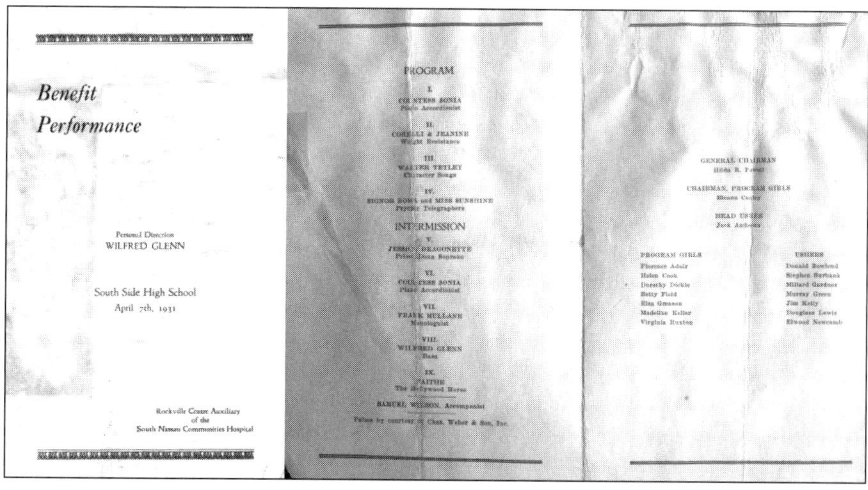

Benefit Performance

Personal Direction
WILFRED GLENN

South Side High School
April 7th, 1931

Rockville Centre Auxiliary
of the
South Nassau Communities Hospital

PROGRAM

I.
COUNTESS SONIA

II.
CORELLI & JEANINE

III.
WALTER TETLEY
Character Songs

IV.
SIGNOR ROMA and MISS SUNSHINE
Psychic Telegraphers

INTERMISSION

V.
JESSICA DRAGONETTE

VI.
COUNTESS SONIA

VII.
FRANK MULLANE
Monologuist

VIII.
WILFRED GLENN
Bass

IX.
FAITHE

SAMUEL WILSON, Accompanist

GENERAL CHAIRMAN

CHAIRMAN, PROGRAM GIRLS

HEAD USHER
Jack Anderson

PROGRAM GIRLS

USHERS

POTTSTOWN BAND'S
May Festival of Music

WALTER TETLEY

FEATURING BOY ARTISTS
From The Children's Hour of Station WJZ

WALTER TETLEY
Scotch Comedian

WALTER SCOTT
Violin

WM. F. LAMB, 2nd
Cornet and Marimba

FRITZ STROUSE
Marimba and Chimes

SENIOR HIGH SCHOOL MALE CHORUS
Prof. Jos. A. Sutton, Director

VICTOR THEATRE, POTTSTOWN, PA.
Friday Evening, May 1, 1931, 8.30 o'clock D. S. T.
WM. F. LAMB Conductor

A wee bit of Scotland, circa 1932.

On April 7, 1931 he appeared in a benefit performance for South Side High School in New Jersey for the Rockville Centre Auxiliary of the South Nassau Communities Hospital. He was third on the bill, after a piano accordionist and a "weight resistance" duo, and again performed character songs.

On May 1st he appeared at Pottstown Band's May Festival of Music,

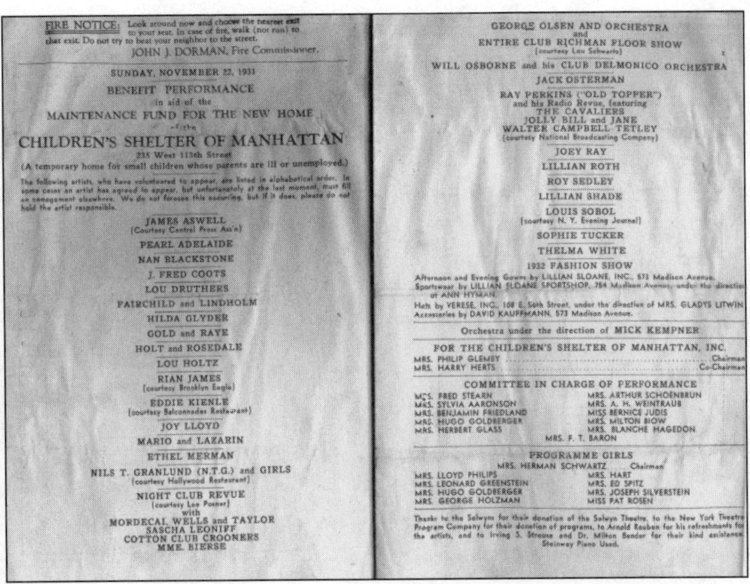

FIRE NOTICE: Look around now and choose the nearest exit to your seat. In case of fire, walk (not run) to that exit. Do not try to beat your neighbor to the street.
JOHN J. DORMAN, Fire Commissioner.

SUNDAY, NOVEMBER 22, 1931

BENEFIT PERFORMANCE
in aid of the
MAINTENANCE FUND FOR THE NEW HOME
of the
CHILDREN'S SHELTER OF MANHATTAN
235 West 113th Street
(A temporary home for small children whose parents are ill or unemployed.)

The following artists, who have volunteered to appear, are listed in alphabetical order. In some cases an artist has agreed to appear, but unfortunately at the last moment, must fill an engagement elsewhere. We do not foresee this occurring, but if it does, please do not hold the artist responsible.

JAMES ASWELL
(Courtesy Central Press Ass'n)

PEARL ADELAIDE

NAN BLACKSTONE

J. FRED COOTS

LOU DRUTHERS

FAIRCHILD and LINDHOLM

HILDA GLYDER

GOLD and RAYE

HOLT and ROSEDALE

LOU HOLTZ

RIAN JAMES
(courtesy Brooklyn Eagle)

EDDIE KIENLE
(courtesy Balconnades Restaurant)

JOY LLOYD

MARIO and LAZARIN

ETHEL MERMAN

NILS T. GRANLUND (N.T.G.) and GIRLS
(courtesy Hollywood Restaurant)

NIGHT CLUB REVUE
(courtesy Lee Posner)
with
MORDECAI, WELLS and TAYLOR
SASCHA LEONIFF
COTTON CLUB CROONERS
MME. BIERSE

GEORGE OLSEN AND ORCHESTRA
and
ENTIRE CLUB RICHMAN FLOOR SHOW
(courtesy Lou Schwartz)

WILL OSBORNE and his CLUB DELMONICO ORCHESTRA

JACK OSTERMAN

RAY PERKINS ("OLD TOPPER")
and his Radio Revue, featuring
THE CAVALIERS
JOLLY BILL and JANE
WALTER CAMPBELL TETLEY
(courtesy National Broadcasting Company)

JOEY RAY

LILLIAN ROTH

ROY SEDLEY

LILLIAN SHADE

LOUIS SOBOL
(courtesy N. Y. Evening Journal)

SOPHIE TUCKER

THELMA WHITE

1932 FASHION SHOW

Afternoon and Evening Gowns by LILLIAN SLOANE, INC., 573 Madison Avenue.
Sportswear by LILLIAN SLOANE SPORTSHOP, 754 Madison Avenue, under the direction of ANN HYMAN.
Hats by VERESE, INC., 108 E. 56th Street, under the direction of MRS. GLADYS LITWIN
Accessories by DAVID KAUFFMANN, 573 Madison Avenue.

Orchestra under the direction of MICK KEMPNER

FOR THE CHILDREN'S SHELTER OF MANHATTAN, INC.

MRS. PHILIP GLEMBY .... Chairman
MRS. HARRY HERTS .... Co-Chairman

COMMITTEE IN CHARGE OF PERFORMANCE

MRS. FRED STEARN — MRS. ARTHUR SCHOENBRUN
MRS. SYLVIA AARONSON — MRS. A. H. WEINTRAUB
MRS. BENJAMIN FRIEDLAND — MISS BERNICE JUDIS
MRS. HUGO GOLDBERGER — MRS. MILTON BIOW
MRS. HERBERT GLASS — MRS. BLANCHE HAGEDON
MRS. F. T. BARON

PROGRAMME GIRLS

MRS. HERMAN SCHWARTZ Chairman

MRS. LLOYD PHILIPS — MRS. HART
MRS. LEONARD GREENSTEIN — MRS. ED SPITZ
MRS. HUGO GOLDBERGER — MRS. JOSEPH SILVERSTEIN
MRS. GEORGE HOLZMAN — MISS PAT ROSEN

Thanks to the Selwyns for their donation of the Selwyn Theatre, to the New York Theatre Program Company for their donation of programs, to Arnold Reuben for his refreshments for the artists, and to Irving S. Strouse and Dr. Milton Bender for their kind assistance.
Steinway Piano Used.

FRANK HAGUE

December 3, 1931.

Dear Mr. Tetley:

May I hope that word of my appreciation for the prompt response and generous aid you gave our Midnight Shows for the unemployed on Thanksgiving Eve may be a slight recompense for the substantial and unselfish contribution you made to their success?

The entertainment was delightful and the financial returns exceeded our highest expectations.

Thanking you again, believe me,

Sincerely,

Frank Hague

Mayor.

Mr. Walter Campbell Tetley,
740 Riverside Drive,
New York City.

5c
Per Copy

What's On The Air

WEEK OF JULY 26, 1931

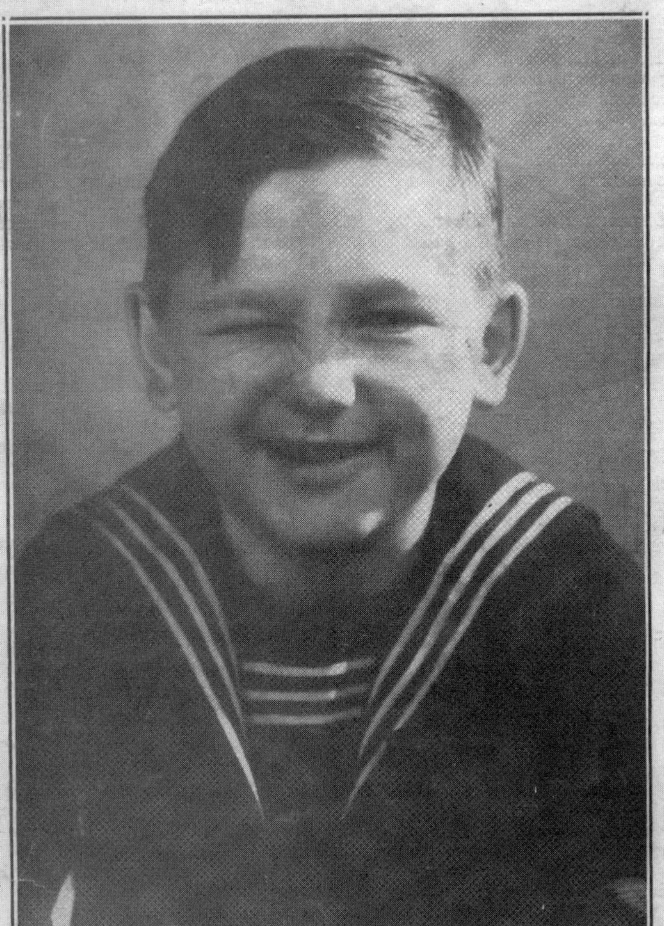

Walter Campbell Tetley—Juvenile Star
(Story on Page 21)

"featuring boy artists from *The Children's Hour* of Station WJZ." At 8:30 p.m. in the Victor Theatre in Pottstown, Pennsylvania, a musical evening ensued, led by conductor William F. Lamb, who also played cornet and marimba.

Tetley appeared at Stevens Memorial Hall "under the management of NBC Artists Service" on May 14, 1931. He was hailed as "the star performer in the Clan MacLennan concert" to journalists. He even appeared at the fourth birthday party of the Edgewater Chapter O.E.S. in a parish house.

He was usually managed by Frances Rockefeller King of the Private Entertainment Department of the National Broadcasting Company, and later on by NBC Artists Service, George Engles, managing director. NBC was aggressively marketing their little star; they knew it would only help their shows, too. The headline of one ad instructed event leaders that they could have "a wee bit of Scotch for your next show," and pressed the point home that a child star was cheaper than a full-grown one: "Enjoy big entertainment by a small star at a small price. This thirteen-year-old radio star is a thrifty buy. A rare comedian who will brighten any entertainment and has a repertoire as extensive as most adult performers." It was a campaign that continued to pay off, for star and studio both.

Mrs. Tetley was not at all pleased that many of the people who wrote about her talented young son constantly referred to him, his songs, and even his nationality, as being "Scotch." "*Scotch*," she insisted, "is a *whiskey—not* a *nationality*." She was Scottish and proud of it—and wanted the world to know.

Proof that constant publicity can be very effective became quite evident during the last week of July 1931 when Walter's cheerful face with its grin that would never wear out, smiled and winked at the world from the cover of a weekly publication that sold for five cents, *Radiolog*. It gave full

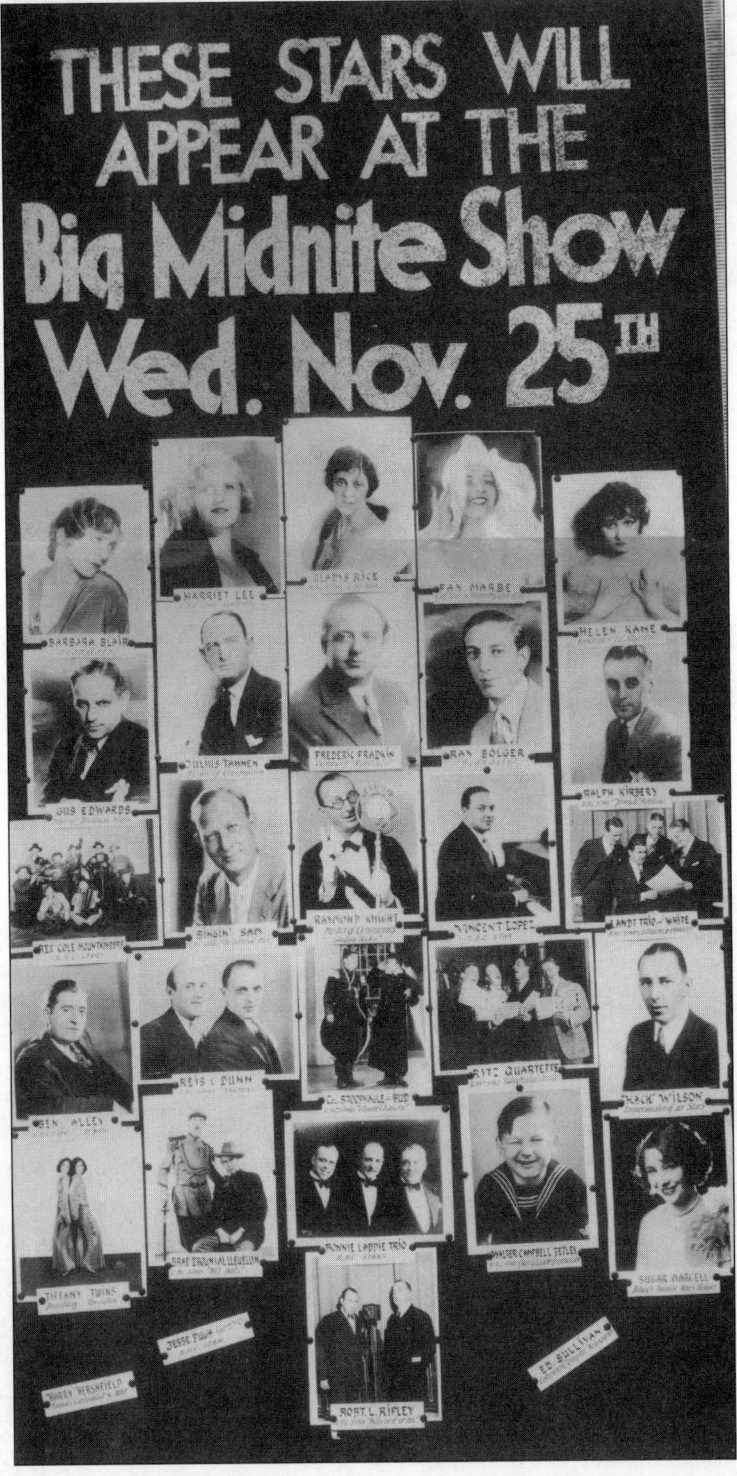
THESE STARS WILL APPEAR AT THE
Big Midnite Show
Wed. Nov. 25TH
HARRIET LEE
GLADYS RICE
FAY MARBE
HELEN KANE
BARBARA BLAIR
JULIUS TANNEN
FREDERIC FRADKIN
RAY BOLGER
RALPH KIRBERY
GUS EDWARDS
REX COLE MOUNTAINEERS
SINGIN' SAM
RAYMOND KNIGHT
VINCENT LOPEZ
REIS & DUNN
RITZ QUARTETTE
BEN ALLEY
TIFFANY TWINS
WALTER CAMPBELL TETLEY
SUGAR MARCELL
ROBT. L. RIPLEY
ED SULLIVAN
HARRY HERSHFIELD

listings of all broadcasts for the current week.

Some of the news items that appeared in the press began to hint that Tetley was "a natural for motion pictures." When it reached Jessie's ears she wanted to be certain that when the opportunity presented itself, he would be ready and waiting. She arranged for him to have voice and acting training at Hugh McClarin's studio in Ridgefield.

In November of 1931 Walter was performing "in aid of the maintenance fund for the new home of the Children's Shelter of Manhattan" at the Selwyn Theatre on 235 West 113th Street. Aiding children in need was something he would continue to do for the rest of his life. In this case, young "Walter Campbell Tetley (courtesy National Broadcasting Company)" was joined by a host of luminaries. Lillian Roth, Sophie Tucker, and Thelma White were just a few of the film, radio and stage names that took part.

Another benefit show around this time began at midnight, at the Loew's Theatre in Jersey City on Thanksgiving, 1931. Robert L. "Believe It Or Not" Ripley, Ray Bolger, Ed Sullivan, Helen Kane and at least twenty other acts joined Walter for the ambitious production which benefited National Motion Picture Week for Local Unemployment Relief, sponsored by Mayor Frank Hague. On the following December 2nd Walter received a letter of thanks at his 740 Riverside Drive residence in New York City:

"Words are puny things when one attempts to express gratitude for such kind cooperation as you recently gave us. It was splendid, and I know all Jersey City would tell you the same thing, were it able to make itself heard.

"It was a source of great satisfaction to all of us and I am sure it will be to you, when I tell you the police report that twenty-five hundred persons were turned away from the theatre. Incidentally, our show at Loew's Jersey City was the only one in the city that played to capacity house.

"I hope that we did not cause you to lose too much sleep and rest assured that I feel so deeply obligated to you that I won't impose upon your good nature again for a long time.

"With every good wish for your future success, I am

"Sincerely yours,

"S. Jay"

A letter from Mayor Frank Hague also came before Christmas, ending with "the entertainment was delightful and the financial returns exceeded our highest expectations."

CHAPTER 3

It's been said that by the time Walter was sixteen (1931) he had made 3,250 radio appearances. Most of these shows no longer exist. Some credits recorded in the little black notebook only gave the name "Records," which more than likely meant transcription discs recorded for later broadcast. Unfortunately, Walter's parents did not indicate what these "Records" were, shrouding his credit list in further mystery.

On March 11, 1931 NBC released a press statement proclaiming their little star had had his contract renewed for two more years. He traveled extensively in the Eastern states between radio dates. Pottstown, Pennsylvania, Yonkers, New York, Scranton, Pennsylvania, Trenton, New Jersey, Washington, D.C., and many other theatres and civic clubs were just a train journey away.

At a Sunday school picnic at Central Park in Allentown, Pennsylvania on July 16, 1931 Walter appeared and sang several of his most popu-

1931 **ANNUAL PICNIC** 1931

St. Paul's Lutheran Sunday School

South Eighth Street :: Allentown, Pa.

Central Park--Thursday, July 16, 1931

Featuring

Free Milk

Ice Cream

Lolly Pops

Games

Contests

Specialties

WALTER CAMPBELL TETLEY

("Wee Sir Harry Lauder")

The fourteen-year-old entertainer; well known on the Children's Hour from WJZ, will be with us in person; dressed in his Kilts, etc. You will have him with you all day and evening. This charming little fellow will sing for you both afternoon and evening. Paul Held will be his accompanist.

COME TO THE PICNIC — BRING YOUR FRIENDS — EVERYBODY WELCOME

We want as many as possible to be at the Park not later than 1.30 P.M. We will be in the lower Grove, near the Baseball Diamond.

(MASTER TETLEY IS PRESENTED THRU THE COURTESY OF THE NATIONAL BROADCASTING CO. ARTISTS SERVICE)

The Edgewater, New Jersey home.

lar numbers. Advance publicity declared: "You'll like him and his Scotch songs. Don't forget the date. We want the biggest turnout we've ever had." The picnic committee chairman had met with the young star weeks before the event at WJZ studios and found the young lad to be "astoundingly bright for a boy of not quite fourteen years of age" and "that he has remained entirely unspoiled and wholesome despite the fact that he has received national recognition for his talent." A leaflet which was handed liberally around proclaimed, "The fourteen-year-old entertainer, well-known on *The Children's Hour* from WJZ, will be with us in person, dressed in his Kilts, etc. You will have him with you all day and evening. This charming little fellow will sing for you both afternoon and evening. Paul

Catching the ferry to work.

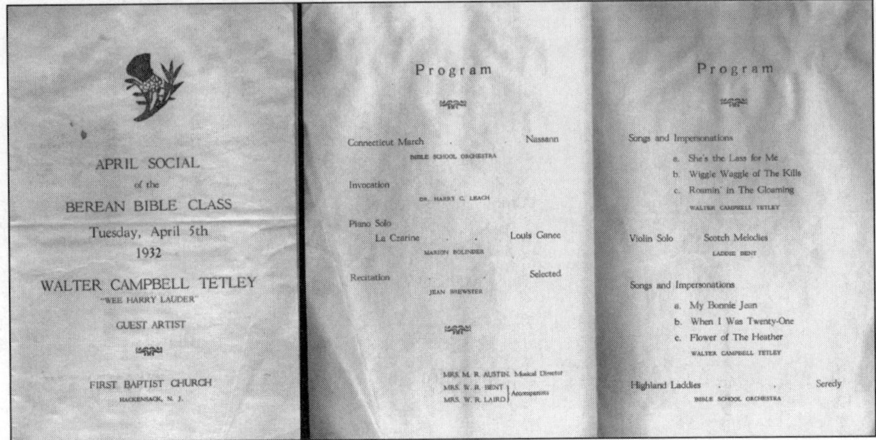

APRIL SOCIAL
of the
BEREAN BIBLE CLASS
Tuesday, April 5th
1932

WALTER CAMPBELL TETLEY
"WEE HARRY LAUDER"

GUEST ARTIST

FIRST BAPTIST CHURCH
HACKENSACK, N. J.

Program

Connecticut March . . Nassann
BIBLE SCHOOL ORCHESTRA

Invocation
DR. HARRY C. LEACH

Piano Solo
La Czarine . . Louis Ganee
MARION BOLINDER

Recitation . . Selected
JEAN BREWSTER

MRS. M. R. AUSTIN, Musical Director
MRS. W. R. BENT, MRS. W. R. LAIRD — Accompanists

Program

Songs and Impersonations
a. She's the Lass for Me
b. Wiggle Waggle of The Kilts
c. Roamin' in The Gloaming
WALTER CAMPBELL TETLEY

Violin Solo Scotch Melodies
LADDIE BENT

Songs and Impersonations
a. My Bonnie Jean
b. When I Was Twenty-One
c. Flower of The Heather
WALTER CAMPBELL TETLEY

Highland Laddies . . Seredy
BIBLE SCHOOL ORCHESTRA

Held will be his accompanist." FREE MILK, ICE CREAM, LOLLY POPS, GAMES, CONTESTS, SPECIALTIES!

Around this time the Tetleys moved to 13 Adelaide Place in Edgewater, New Jersey. They rented the small seven-room house (and roomy attic) because it was near Fred's post office job. The ferry Walter and his mother always took into New York was also only a short walk away. The boat crossing was at 125th Street and the fare was only a nickel.

At home, Walter kept two tie racks full of already-tied ties. One for everyday work (he was never without a bow or regular tie during working hours), and one group for Sundays. He kept a miniature figure of Captain Henry from his *Show Boat* series on top of the Sunday tie rack.

On April 5, 1932 Walter appeared as guest artist at the April Social of the Berean Bible Class at the First Baptist Church of Hackensack, New Jersey. His songs (about twenty-two numbers) and impersonations included "She's the Lass for Me," "Wiggle Waggle of the Kilt," "Roamin' in the Gloaming," "My Bonnie Jean," "When I was Twenty-One," and "Flower of the Heather."

Walter and friends.

These were adult-type songs, to be

sure, but they were the staples of his act, which he performed time and again. Such as at the Mother and Daughter Banquet at the Presbyterian Church in Morris Plains, New Jersey. The local paper called him the "bright spot" of the evening and wrote that he was "popular with everyone."

Walter and mother Tetley.

A Coaldale, Pennsylvania newspaper devoted an entire column to Walter's upcoming April 15th performance at the Coaldale High School Auditorium in aid of the Auspices Coaldale Relief Society. He appeared with two other *Children's Hour* stars. It's difficult to say how much of the highly complimentary write-up was true, but it was great publicity to say that Walter studied algebra, French, English and Civics at "a Professional Children's School in New York." He listed his hobbies as reading, especially the mystery thriller type (tops was Sherlock Holmes), and playing baseball. "I played baseball often. There were plenty of open spaces where we lived in New Jersey. I played pitcher and first base. Gee, I could throw curves, drops, slow balls and everything!"

He was usually catcher or first baseman in the game, when time allowed. He also enjoyed a good game of football with friends, though he had more time for a game of marbles in the studio between shows. He also collected match-covers—over 500 by August of 1937—and kept tropical fish, and dogs. Scrappy, his wire-haired terrier, came from a New Jersey kennel and cost $35. Sandy, a Scotch (of course!) terrier, cost $25 from a Brooklyn kennel. Both were thoroughbreds, though Walter's strong sense of charity would never have him buy a "designer" dog from a posh seller at a terrible price when there were poor dogs in need out there.

He also liked to carve and make items out of wood.

Almost all radio stars at the time were endorsing commercial items of some kind. Most of the time it was cigarettes. Young Walter was ap-

N. B. C. CHILDREN'S HOUR CONCERT

Auspices Coaldale Relief Society
FRIDAY, EVENING APRIL 15, 1932

PROGRAMME.

COALDALE HIGH SCHOOL BAND.

(a) March: Spirit of Coaldale High ....John J. Horn
(b) Overture: Gypsy Festival ....Al Hayes

WALTER SCOTT

(a) Pampourin Chinois ....Kreisler
(b) Caprice Vienois ....Kreisler
(c) The Swan ....Saint-Saens
(d) Liebesfreud ....Kreisler

PEGGY ZINKE

First Appearance ....Dutch Impersonations

WALTER TETLEY

(a) She's The Lass for Me.
(b) Wiggle Waggle of the Kill.

PEGGY ZINKE

Second Appearance ....French Impersonations

COALDALE HIGH SCHOOL BAND.

(a) First Movement Unfinished Symphony ....Schubert
(b) March: Good Fellowship ....F. O. Griffin

WALTER TETLEY

(a) When I Was Twenty-One.
(b) My Bonnie Jean.

PEGGY ZINKE

Third Appearance ....Irish Impersonations

WALTER SCOTT

(a) Hungarian Dance No. 1 ....Brahms
(b) Old Refrain ....Kreisler
(c) Valse Staccato ....Borrisosn
(d) Dance of The Goblins ....Bazzinni

PEGGY ZINKE

Fourth Appearance ....Readings

WALTER TETLEY

(a) Flower of the Heather.
(b) The Message Boy.

COALDALE HIGH SCHOOL BAND.

(a) Overture Mount Everest ....F. O. Griffin
(b) Stars and Stripes Forever ....Sousa

"Star Spangled Banner."

Accompanist—Richard Brimble.

proached by the makers of Tootsie Rolls for a variety of magazine ads featuring the cameral product. "Radio stars, movies stars—men, women and children all over the country go for them in a big way. Have *you* tried a Tootsie today?" One later such advertisement appeared on the back cover of the July 24, 1937 issue of *Radio Guide*. That same magazine used another spread—with a different Tetley picture—also featuring Gus Arnheim and Jane Pickens in the August 14th issue, which hit

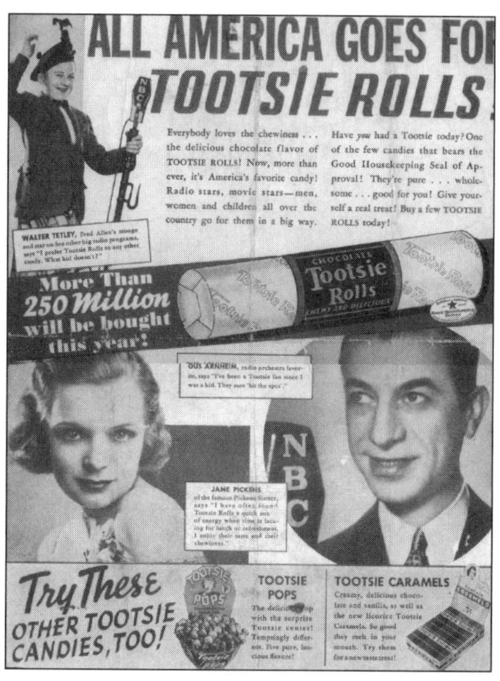

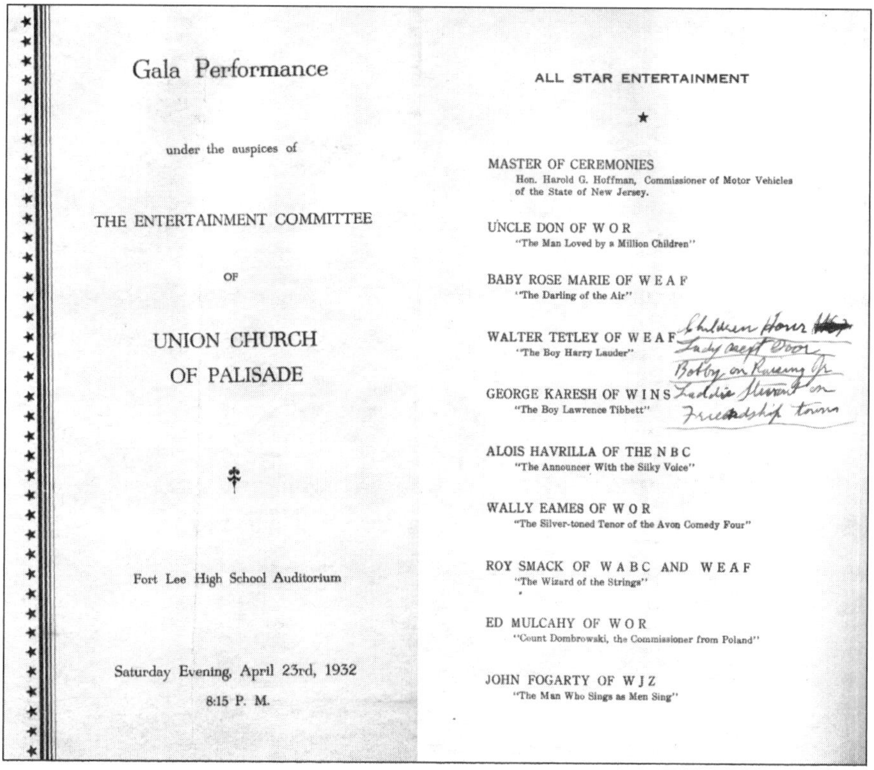

Gala Performance

under the auspices of

THE ENTERTAINMENT COMMITTEE

OF

UNION CHURCH
OF PALISADE

Fort Lee High School Auditorium

Saturday Evening, April 23rd, 1932
8:15 P. M.

ALL STAR ENTERTAINMENT

★

MASTER OF CEREMONIES
Hon. Harold G. Hoffman, Commissioner of Motor Vehicles of the State of New Jersey.

UNCLE DON OF W O R
"The Man Loved by a Million Children"

BABY ROSE MARIE OF W E A F
"The Darling of the Air"

WALTER TETLEY OF W E A F
"The Boy Harry Lauder"

Children Hour ~~WOR~~
Lady Next Door
Bobby on Raising Jr
Laddie Stewart on
Friendship town

GEORGE KARESH OF W I N S
"The Boy Lawrence Tibbett"

ALOIS HAVRILLA OF THE N B C
"The Announcer With the Silky Voice"

WALLY EAMES OF W O R
"The Silver-toned Tenor of the Avon Comedy Four"

ROY SMACK OF W A B C AND W E A F
"The Wizard of the Strings"

ED MULCAHY OF W O R
"Count Dombrowski, the Commissioner from Poland"

JOHN FOGARTY OF W J Z
"The Man Who Sings as Men Sing"

ATTRACTIONS
DEC. 27th to JAN. 2nd

CAPITOL
THEATRE
BAYSIDE, L. I.

Telephone: BAyside 9—6517

Matinee Saturday, Sunday and Holidays

REDUCED PRICES!

Weekday Evenings

CHILDREN 15c
ADULTS 25c

Saturday, Sunday and Holiday Evenings

CHILDREN 15c
ADULTS 30c

ALWAYS A DOUBLE FEATURE ALL - TALKING PROGRAM!

A Merry Christmas and a Very Happy New Year To All

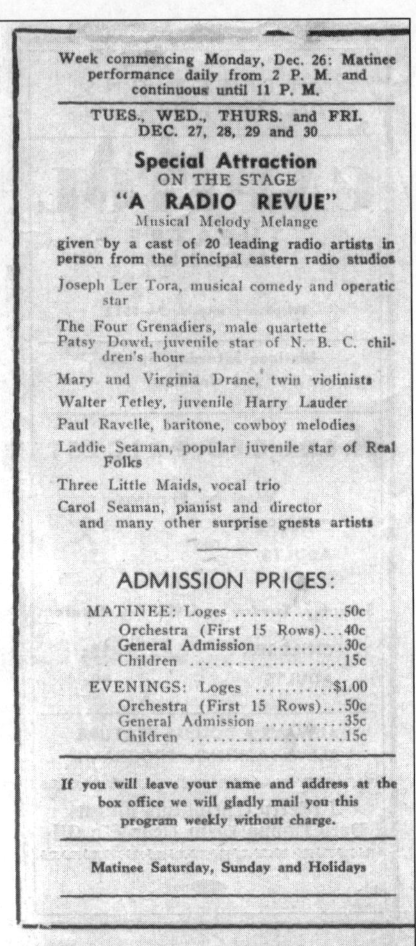

Week commencing Monday, Dec. 26: Matinee performance daily from 2 P. M. and continuous until 11 P. M.

TUES., WED., THURS. and FRI.
DEC. 27, 28, 29 and 30

Special Attraction
ON THE STAGE
"A RADIO REVUE"
Musical Melody Melange

given by a cast of 20 leading radio artists in person from the principal eastern radio studios

Joseph Ler Tora, musical comedy and operatic star

The Four Grenadiers, male quartette

Patsy Dowd, juvenile star of N. B. C. children's hour

Mary and Virginia Drane, twin violinists

Walter Tetley, juvenile Harry Lauder

Paul Ravelle, baritone, cowboy melodies

Laddie Seaman, popular juvenile star of Real Folks

Three Little Maids, vocal trio

Carol Seaman, pianist and director
and many other surprise guests artists

ADMISSION PRICES:

MATINEE: Loges 50c
Orchestra (First 15 Rows) ... 40c
General Admission 30c
Children 15c

EVENINGS: Loges $1.00
Orchestra (First 15 Rows) ... 50c
General Admission 35c
Children 15c

If you will leave your name and address at the box office we will gladly mail you this program weekly without charge.

Matinee Saturday, Sunday and Holidays

newsstands on August 5th. It showed Walter in Scottish garb smiling and holding the NBC microphone. Along with a nice sized check, he was sent a box of Tootsie Rolls in appreciation.

Back in the studio, Walter was earning himself a reputation as a good supporting player to have around. One early radio review, probably in 1932, singled Walter out for his "astounding performance in a thrilling murder mystery drama to be sent over the air today and tomorrow. The sketch is an adaptation of a true story in *The American Weekly*. It concerns a series of mysterious killings in which children are poisoned in their nurseries by a strange gas which is forced into the room."

And the personal appearances helped keep Walter Tetley's name on listeners' minds. On April 22, 1932 Walter sang his usual songs at a concert, directed by William R. Reese, at the Memorial High School audito-

WALTER CAMPBELL TETLEY

Walter Campbell Tetley, the "Wee Sir Harry Lauder" of radio and vaudeville, has been heard for the last year from Station WJZ in the programs "The Lady Next Door" and "The Children's Hour." Only twelve years old, Walter has been singing since he was five and has been entertaining professionally since he entered vaudeville at the age of seven, doing his imitation of the songs of Sir Harry Lauder. His greatest thrill was when he met and had luncheon with Sir Harry two years ago and was nicknamed "Wee Sir Harry" by the famous Scotch comedian.

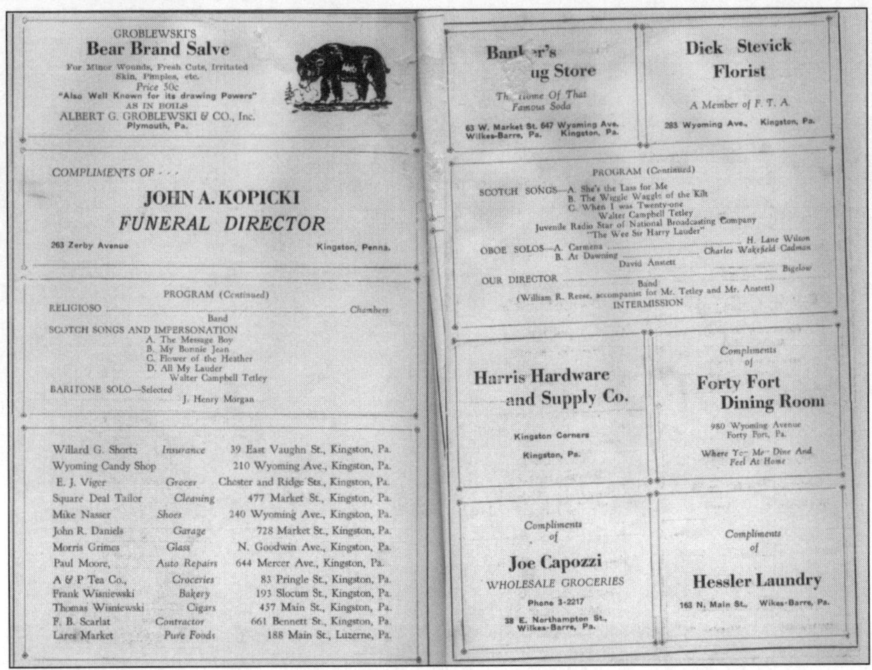

GROBLEWSKI'S
Bear Brand Salve
For Minor Wounds, Fresh Cuts, Irritated Skin, Pimples, etc.
Price 50c
"Also Well Known for its drawing Powers"
AS IN BOILS
ALBERT G. GROBLEWSKI & CO., Inc.
Plymouth, Pa.

COMPLIMENTS OF - - -
JOHN A. KOPICKI
FUNERAL DIRECTOR
263 Zerby Avenue Kingston, Penna.

PROGRAM (Continued)

RELIGIOSO .... *Chambers*
Band

SCOTCH SONGS AND IMPERSONATION
A. The Message Boy
B. My Bonnie Jean
C. Flower of the Heather
D. All My Lauder
Walter Campbell Tetley

BARITONE SOLO—Selected
J. Henry Morgan

Willard G. Shortz	*Insurance*	39 East Vaughn St., Kingston, Pa.
Wyoming Candy Shop		210 Wyoming Ave., Kingston, Pa.
E. J. Viger	*Grocer*	Chester and Ridge Sts., Kingston, Pa.
Square Deal Tailor	*Cleaning*	477 Market St., Kingston, Pa.
Mike Nasser	*Shoes*	240 Wyoming Ave., Kingston, Pa.
John R. Daniels	*Garage*	728 Market St., Kingston, Pa.
Morris Grimes	*Glass*	N. Goodwin Ave., Kingston, Pa.
Paul Moore,	*Auto Repairs*	644 Mercer Ave., Kingston, Pa.
A & P Tea Co.,	*Groceries*	83 Pringle St., Kingston, Pa.
Frank Wisniewski	*Bakery*	193 Slocum St., Kingston, Pa.
Thomas Wisniewski	*Cigars*	457 Main St., Kingston, Pa.
F. B. Scarlat	*Contractor*	661 Bennett St., Kingston, Pa.
Lares Market	*Pure Foods*	188 Main St., Luzerne, Pa.

Ban[illegible]r's [illegible]ug Store
Th[illegible] Home Of That Famous Soda
63 W. Market St. Wilkes-Barre, Pa. 647 Wyoming Ave. Kingston, Pa.

Dick Stevick Florist
A Member of F. T. A.
283 Wyoming Ave., Kingston, Pa.

PROGRAM (Continued)

SCOTCH SONGS—A. She's the Lass for Me
B. The Wiggle Waggle of the Kilt
C. When I was Twenty-one
Walter Campbell Tetley
Juvenile Radio Star of National Broadcasting Company
"The Wee Sir Harry Lauder"

OBOE SOLOS—A. Carmena .... *H. Lane Wilson*
B. At Dawning .... *Charles Wakefield Cadman*
David Anstett

OUR DIRECTOR .... Bigelow
Band

(William R. Reese, accompanist for Mr. Tetley and Mr. Anstett)

INTERMISSION

Harris Hardware and Supply Co.
Kingston Corners
Kingston, Pa.

Compliments of
Forty Fort Dining Room
980 Wyoming Avenue
Forty Fort, Pa.
Where Yo[illegible] Me[illegible] Dine And Feel At Home

Compliments of
Joe Capozzi
WHOLESALE GROCERIES
Phone 3-2217
38 E. Northampton St.,
Wilkes-Barre, Pa.

Compliments of
Hessler Laundry
163 N. Main St., Wikes-Barre, Pa.

rium in Kingston, Pennsylvania. As always, he was a smash.

The following night he appeared at a "Gala Performance under the auspices of the Entertainment Committee of Union Church of Palisade" at Fort Lee High School Auditorium, with Baby Rose Marie (of WEAF), Uncle Don (of WOR) and other radio acts. The Master of Ceremonies was the Honorable Harold G. Hoffman, Commissioner of Motor Vehicles of the State of New Jersey. The 8:15 p.m. Saturday night performance was followed by dancing.

For a whole quarter patrons could witness a "one-act play and chorus selections by members of the choir" with "assisting artists: Walter Tetley, well-known radio artist and star; Miss Grace Lang, 15-year-old Chinese pianist and winner in musical contests; Miss Vivian Donaldson, harpist" and others. Musical selections were played by the Edgewater Symphony Orchestra. The evening began at 8:15 p.m. on Thursday, June 7th at the Eleanor Van Gelder School.

Back on March 4, 1932 Walter had first appeared on *Friendship Town* as Laddie Stewart. Later that year, he got himself a "big sister" by the name of Margaret Stewart. She was brought in to perform Scottish, Irish and French songs. Harry Salter and his orchestra performed music for the series. The program was sponsored by the Chesebrough Manufacturing Company, which had a brief run on CBS, but quickly came back to NBC.

Walter shared the bill for the "N.B.C. Children's Hour Concert" with Peggy Zinke and Walter Scott. Tetley again performed his usual musical fare: "She's the Lass For Me," "Wiggle Waggle of the Kilt," "My Bonnie Jean," "When I Was Twenty-One," "Flower of the Heather," and also "The Message Boy." The review which followed the concert stated that the troupe "proved equal to any entertainers that ever visited the valley, and they met with wonderful success."

Walter Tetley ended 1932 by joining in a week-long run of "A Radio Review, a musical melody melange" given at the Capitol Theatre in Bayside, New York on December 27-30. He joined "a cast of 20 leading radio artists in person from the principal eastern radio studios," including musical comedy and operatic star Joseph Lertora, a male quartette called The Four Grenadiers, the twin violists Mary and Virginia Dran, the vocal trio Three Little Maids, and others. Matinees were given daily beginning at 2 p.m. until 11 p.m.

From sharing so much limelight with his contemporaries it was obvious that fame was taking a long time to get to the little star's head. He never did become a "fat head."

CHAPTER 4

Not just the personal appearances, but the travel time involved took up a lot of Tetley's off-hours from radio. He appeared in a Woodland Hills, Pennsylvania variety show where he was once again singled out by the local reviewer. "On Sunday evening, a real treat is promised when Walter Tetley, the world's foremost juvenile Scottish entertainer will appear. This artist needs little introduction…"

By now he was a national name, though still a supporting player on radio. It was rumored that he had signed up for an extended vaudeville tour near the end of 1932, but his continuing radio work showed no signs

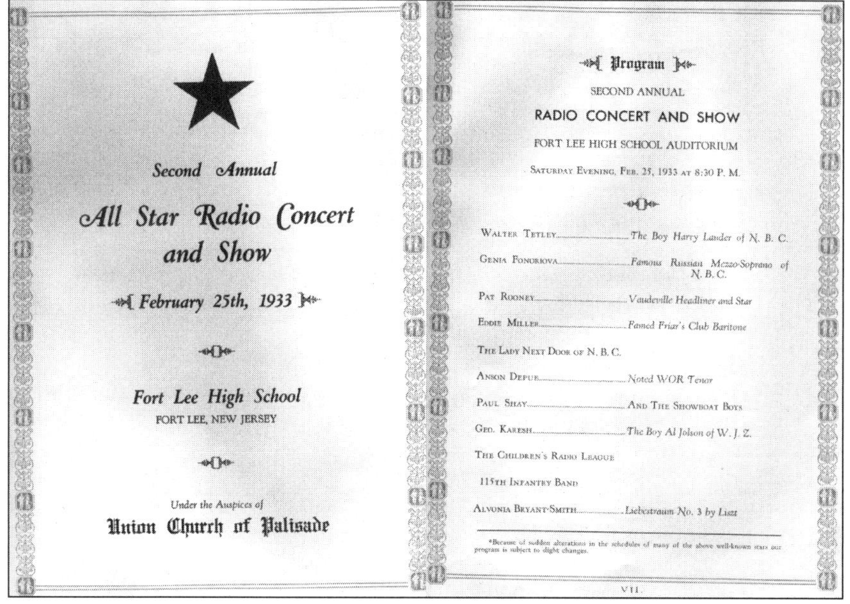

Second Annual

All Star Radio Concert and Show

February 25th, 1933

Fort Lee High School

FORT LEE, NEW JERSEY

Under the Auspices of

Union Church of Palisade

Program

SECOND ANNUAL

RADIO CONCERT AND SHOW

FORT LEE HIGH SCHOOL AUDITORIUM

SATURDAY EVENING, FEB. 25, 1933 AT 8:30 P. M.

WALTER TETLEY........ *The Boy Harry Lauder of N. B. C.*

GENIA FONORIOVA........ *Famous Russian Mezzo-Soprano of N. B. C.*

PAT ROONEY........ *Vaudeville Headliner and Star*

EDDIE MILLER........ *Famed Friar's Club Baritone*

THE LADY NEXT DOOR OF N. B. C.

ANSON DEPUE........ *Noted WOR Tenor*

PAUL SHAY........ AND THE SHOWBOAT BOYS

GEO. KARESH........ *The Boy Al Jolson of W. J. Z.*

THE CHILDREN'S RADIO LEAGUE

115TH INFANTRY BAND

ALVONIA BRYANT-SMITH........ *Liebestraum No. 3 by Liszt*

*Because of sudden alterations in the schedules of many of the above well-known stars our program is subject to slight changes.

VII.

NBC-RKO

Presents

"THE R. K. OLIANS"

Mr. Harry Meyer - - - - - - - Conductor

Walter Campbell Tetley - - - - - - Guest Artist

Under direction of - - - Frances Rockefeller King

— DANCE ORDER —

1—Fox Trot—"Rise'n Shine" from "Take a Chance" ... Youmans

2—Fox Trot—"If I Ever Get a Job Again" ... Baer

3—Fox Trot—"My Darling" ... Myers

4—Fox Trot—"Fit As a Fiddle" ... Goodhart

5—Waltz —"Gems from 'Melody'" ... Romberg

6—Fox Trot—"You'll Get By" ... Coots

7—Fox Trot—"At the Baby Parade" ... Schuster

8—Fox Trot—"So I Married the Girl" ... Stept

9—Fox Trot—"Louisiana Hayride" from "Flying Colors" ... Schwarts

10—Waltz —"A Boy and a Girl Were Dancing" ... Revel

11—Fox Trot—"Love Me Tonight" ... Rodgers

12—Fox Trot—"Night and Day" from "Gay Divorce" ... Porter

13—Fox Trot—"Sittin' by the Fire With You" ... Wendling

14—Fox Trot—"Hey! Young Feller" ... McHugh

15—Waltz —"Play Fiddle Play" ... Altman

16—Fox Trot—"Every Little Star" from "Music in the Air" Kern

INTERMISSION

17—Fox Trot—"Hits" from "Pardon My English" ... Gershwin

18—Fox Trot—"Moon Song" ... Johnston

19—Fox Trot—"Playing with Fire" ... Berlin

20—Waltz —"Rock-a-Bye Moon" ... Lang

21—Fox Trot—"Here It is Monday" ... Cleary

22—Fox Trot—"Seven Little Steps to Heaven" ... Gensler

23—Fox Trot—"Willow Weep For Me" ... Ahlert

24—Waltz —"I Wake Up Smiling" ... Hupfeld

25—Fox Trot—"Just So You'll Remember" ... Meyer

of slowing down.

Walter took part in an NBC-RKO extravaganza for the stage called *The R. K. Olians*, which featured mostly dancing (almost all fox trots with a few waltzes sprinkled in for variety's sake). Walter Campbell Tetley, under the direction of Frances Rockefeller King, was guest artist. Mr. Harry Meyer conducted the massive music show.

Around the same time, the second annual All-Star Radio Concert and Show was given on February 25, 1933 at Fort Lee High School in Fort Lee, New Jersey. It featured several NBC stars of the day, including Walter, baritone singer Phil Dewey, Genia Fonoriova ("famous Russian Mezzo-Soprano"), and "The Lady Next Door" herself (though she received no name credit; an odd bit of promotion that NBC would also do to Hal Peary). Dancers, singers, comedians, the 115th Infantry Band, the Children's Radio League and other artists provided a gala evening.

March 8, 1933 was the date Tetley joined the cast of *Buck Rogers*, but it wasn't until October 3rd of that year that he became a regular cast member, as "Willie." Walter gave an abundance of auditions in this year, especially in June. The day after one of these the little actor joined the cast of *Winnie-the-Pooh* as the invigorated, bouncy stuffed animal "Tigger." This children's serial was heard over the NBC-WEAF network each Wednesday and Friday at 5:30 p.m. The A.A. Milne stories were adapted by Elizabeth Todd of the NBC continuity department.

At Washington's First Annual Radio and Electric Show that same year Walter was joined by Martha Attwood of the Metropolitan Opera Company, Dr. John Bellamy Taylor (demonstrating his famous "House of Magic," which showed sound waves being converted into light), and master of ceremonies John S. Young, NBC announcer. William S. Abernathy, local WRC announcer, introduced the acts which were also broadcast over WRC. Over 3,500 people attended the first night's show (which Walter did not attend), and over 4,000 the next night. 17-year-old Walter's age was listed as 11 and 12 in several local papers publicizing the event.

Another paper during the same time listed his age as thirteen. It also claimed that "when he is not broadcasting Walter Tetley likes best to climb mountains. But he doesn't have much spare time" due to his three hit series now running simultaneously: *Raising Junior* (over WJZ), *The Children's Hour* (Sunday mornings from 9 to 10, where he sang Scottish songs) and the stalwart *The Lady Next Door*.

Meantime *Buck Rogers* was appealing to critics and audiences alike. One March, 1933 review wrote: "In purchasing this long-run serial Cream of Wheat is making a snappy bid for the kids who go on a hot-cereal diet in winter. *Buck Rogers* has all the trimmings for a two-fisted knockdown, drag-out job. Story, scripted by E.R. Johnstone, fabricates a lot of synthetic adventure which takes place in inter-stellar space 500 years in the future. Lines and pace serve only one purpose—to get as racy as possible—and to that extent admirably suit their ends. Odd voices and weird sound effects (most of the latter poorly done) creep in. Aside from the adventure lure, there is a thick condiment of pseudo-scientific terms." The best component of the series, the reviewer stated, was the cast which "ably sells its stuff the way the layout calls for. Will probably move a good bit of cereal off grocers' shelves."

The commercials themselves were fun. For the price of a box top off a Cream of Wheat box little listeners could join a club to become a "solar scout" and be "a personal friend of Buck Rogers." Members received a gold badge and handbook. Cream of Wheat was touted as "what's needed to succeed."

On July 19, 1933 it was announced to the press that Walter would be playing Stephen Foster (age 6-9) on John Tasker Howard's series on the noted American folksong writer. Broadcast Wednesday evenings on NBC-WEAF at 8:30 p.m. E.S.T., it contained many of Foster's classic melodies as played and sung by an orchestra and quartet directed by NBC music

Tetley playing for corn's sake.

executive Thomas Belviso. Laddie Seaman played the adult Foster. For radio listeners the young actor also portrayed a number of other celebrities during their boyhood days. Among them, sports heroes Babe Ruth and Jack Dempsey, as well as famed actors John and Lionel Barrymore and Richard Barthelmess.

On Maxwell House's *Show Boat* Walter played the blind newsboy waif Eddie, who wandered onto the Showboat and was "adopted" by Lanny Ross and the Show Boat troupe. He began the role on August 24, 1933. Heard over the NBC-WEAF network Thursday nights at 9 p.m., Walter was signed to a 52-week contract for this series. At the same time he signed a 26-week contract to support Helen Hayes in her new radio series which was to commence on October 8th.

Being a typical young boy, in rare free moments away from the microphone, Walter was apt to get into some innocent mischief. If given an opportunity he would hitch a ride atop a piano as it was being moved from studio to studio. Another of his pranks was to find unusual hiding places in the building, such as inside an air-conditioning duct, in the battery room, or control booth, watching the busy engineers work their magic.

But then he found *real* magic in the person of Ray Kelly, chief of the sound effects department. He would often talk to Kelly about the various contraptions he used to produce all the sounds, and relished in being shown examples. Whenever he would walk in for a session of learning, the first thing Walter would do was to blow the huge whistle that opened and closed every *Show Boat* program.

Walter found himself on a series called *Main Street* on September 24, 1933. He would appear on the serial-type show now and then as son Wilbur of the Higgins family. The cast included Don Carney (later famous for his Uncle Don show) as Luke Higgins, Edith Spencer as his wife Sary, Wally Maher as Ezra, Alan Bunce as Jack, Doro Merande as Ivalutty, Robert Strauss as Horace, and Florence Halop as Fanny.

Back in November, 1933 when the network was doing a series of broadcasts of *The Wizard of Oz*, they needed a boy to play the important role of "Tip," so they sent out a casting call. Nearly 100 young actors were auditioned but none were suitable for the role. As was often the case, the casting director turned to a "seasoned workhouse," and got Walter Tetley to do the job. Using his best "12-year-old voice," he took over the role on November 15th.

During the latter half of 1933 when NBC moved to Radio City, Walter appeared as one of the entertainers to launch the new place of business. He was later thanked by John F. Royal of NBC for his "enthusiastic cooperation on the occasion. Our opening week was a great success in no small measure due to your participation." He was also applauded by managing director George Engles: "The spirit which caused you to so unselfishly give of your time, is in my opinion, in keeping with this new era of broadcasting which comes into being with our move to Radio City."

NBC was so proud of their junior star that sometimes they loaned him out to rival networks, as he was in June of 1934 when he "was heard Monday night with the big show over the Columbia broadcasting station with Mady Christian." Also included in the 9:30 p.m. performance were Helen Menken (co-star of *Mary of Scotland*), the "exotic blues singer" Gertrude Niesen, and Erno Rapee and His Orchestra.

1933 came to an end with several other new series for little Tetley. He briefly joined Jane and Goodman Ace in their quarter-hour comedy series, *Easy Aces*; and began *Bobby Benson's Adventures*, also on CBS, on Christmas Eve. Walter appeared as Jock, a Scottish lad, and often appeared in kilt to promote the series. His Scottish photograph was even given away as a radio premium for the series. Though his main appearances were in January of 1934 he would sporadically appear on the series when another youth was needed.

Chapter 5

1934 was a significant year in Walter Tetley's life. On January 4th he had his first appearance with Fred Allen, on the half-hour *Sal Hepatica Revue*. Ultimately Allen was the man who would take Walter to the West Coast where he would remain for the rest of his life.

As one of Allen's Alley Players Walter was signed on in the part of a sassy brat named Waldo. It significantly showed the world that this kid could play comedy. It gave him the perfect venue to showcase his versatility with dialects and character voices and served as a perfect foil to Allen's wry, caustic delivery. Though he was only with the series until the end of 1937, Tetley had picked up a lot of "wise-cracking" skill that would serve him well in future high-profile series.

Town Hall with Fred Allen	The Great Jasper
The Sun	True Story
Uncle Abe & David	Under Wood
Unemployed	Vick Open House
Walter Winchell	Wayside Cottage
Welch with Irene Rich	Wheatenaville
White Owl with Burns & Allen	Winnie the Pooh
Wizard of Oz	Womens Radio Review
Woodbury with Paul Whitemans	Star Dust
Radio Album	

Stars I Work With

Maud Adams	Fred Allen
John Battle	Burns & Allen
Ethel John & Lionel Barrymore	Jack Benny
Louisa M Alcott	Mady Chistians
Eddie Cantor	Clarence Darrow
Jack Dempsey	Spence Dean
Amelia Earhart	Mitzie Green
Block & Sully	Carlson Robinson
Gertrude Niesen	Johnny Hart
George Price	George Jessel
Ripley	Fred Waring
Wheeler & Woolsey	Paul Whiteman
B.A.Rolfe	Leslie Howard
Charles Winninger	Grace Moore
Babe Ruth	Irene Rich
Joe Penner	Jerry Mann
Mary Livingston	Walter Winchell
Marx Brothers	Warden Laws
Sizzlers	Borah Minnevitch
Fred Rich	Lanny Ross
Roxy	George Givot
Guy Lambardo	McIntrye
Raymond Knight	Ace Goodman
Portland Hooper	

The credit list mounts…

On June 30th Tetley's escalating broadcasting career was temporarily halted when he and his mother sailed aboard the *Caledonia* for a seven-week tour of England and Scotland. In lieu of having to pay for their passage, the boy entertained the passengers and crew on both voyages. The enterprising Mrs. Tetley made the special arrangements, and also booked appearance dates in theaters in London, Newcastle, Glasgow,

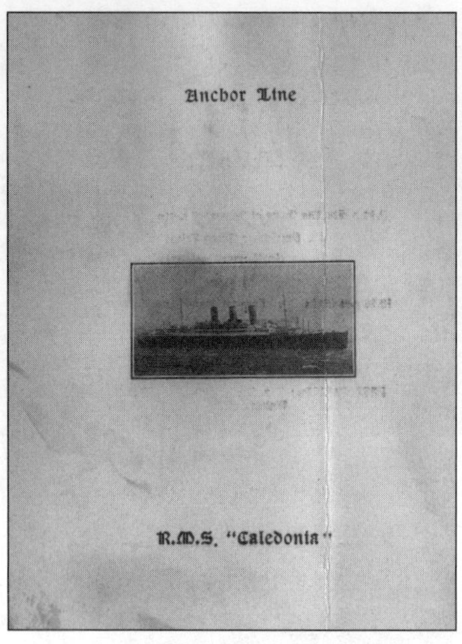

Edinburgh, and elsewhere. The United Kingdom welcomed the lad with open arms and the tour was highly successful. His fame was now international.

Jessie was happy to give her son a more personal tour of many of the cherished landmarks of her homeland. Overall, the tour had been a very enjoyable experience. She had often considered a similar tour across the United States but there was one insurmountable obstacle in her way—the Gerry Society. It was an organization founded in 1875 by a kindly

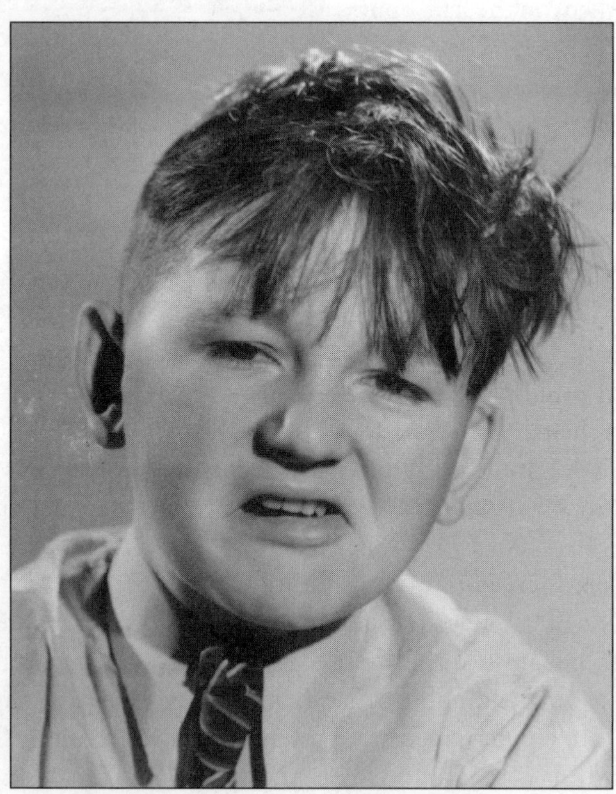

No one played the brat better than Tetley.

CHUM CLUB CERTIFICATE.

DAILY CHUM CLUB RECORD

This is to Certify that

Walter Campbell Tetley

Has on this day, 26th July, 1934 been duly enrolled as a Member of the DAILY RECORD SCOTTISH CHUM CLUB, and has been registered as Chum No. 392455.

(Signed) Uncle Jack

RULES.

1. A Chum is bright and cheerful.
2. A Chum is thoughtful of others.
3. A Chum tries to help those less fortunate or in trouble.
4. A Chum does his or her best to assist the Chum Club schemes.
5. A Chum is always kind to animals, and protects them from ill-treatment.
6. A Chum resolves to do his or her best for Scotland.

The Rules of the Chum Club are simple and few, And easy to keep if you're honest and true.

gentleman named Henry Bergh who was greatly opposed to child labor. The Gerry Society was also known as "The New York Society for the Prevention of Cruelty to Children." Although she could be a formidable foe, Mrs. Tetley did not want to launch a battle with the Gerry Society.

Because of his frequent appearances wearing a kilt, on July 26, 1934 Walter was given honorary membership in "The Scottish Chum Club," and was registered as Chum No. 392455. He was very proud to join the ranks of such other honorary members as Sir Harry Lauder himself.

Membership in the club involved a number of very important rules:

1. A Chum is bright and cheerful.
2. A Chum is thoughtful of others.
3. A Chum tries to help those less fortunate or in trouble.
4. A Chum does his or her best to assist the Chum Club schemes.
5. A Chum is always kind to animals, and protects them from ill-treatment.
6. A Chum resolves to do his or her best for Scotland.

"The Rules of the Chum Club are simple and few. And easy to keep if you're honest and true." Anyone who followed Walter's rigorous charity performances knew that Walter fit right in on those counts.

On the return trip of August 15th Walter joined other entertainers (Rev. Father Bell, Miss M. Prunty and Mr. H. Hammond) for a program of fun, variety and dancing aboard the *H.M.S. Caledonia*. Messrs. Black and Hughan were emcees for the gay cruise which also sported a buffet supper of sandwiches, hot dogs, and ice cream and wafers.

Naturally, Walter's first radio credit upon returning to work on August 18th was *Lady Next Door*. Many more episodes of *The Children's Hour, Fred Allen, Buck Rogers, Eno Crime Club*, auditions and other shows followed.

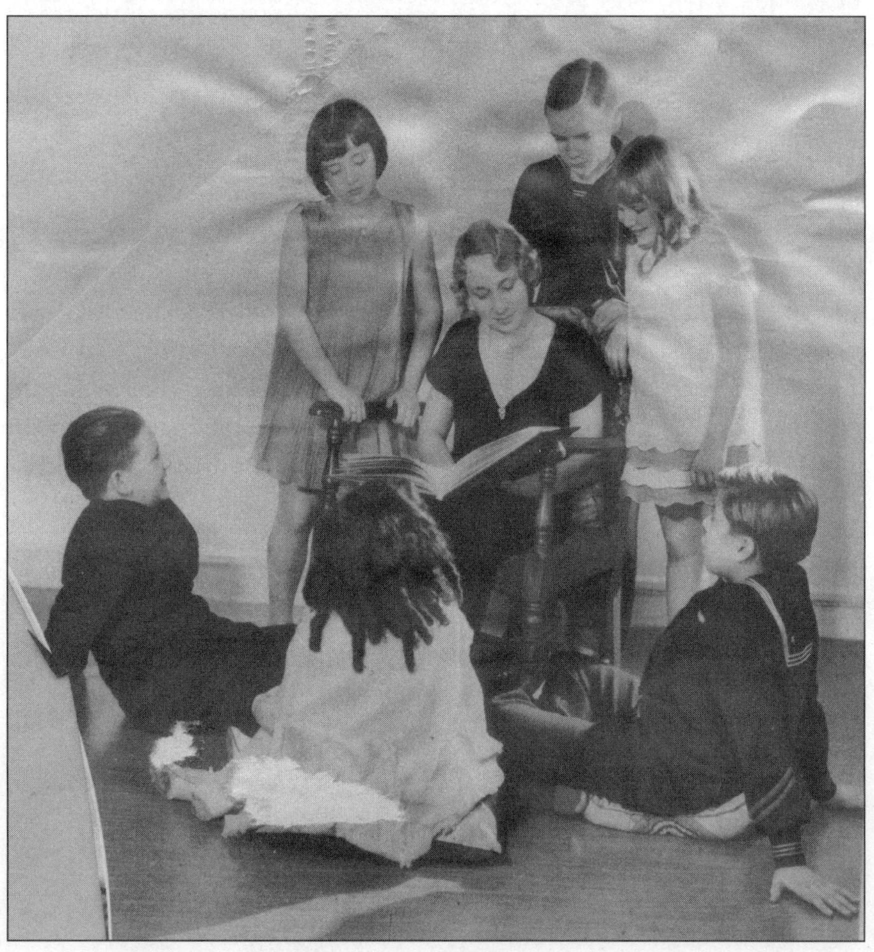

The Lady Next Door, *Madge Tucker, reads to some of her young protegés. Walter sits on floor, left.*

Apart from a successful tour, Walter also came back with gold in hand, in the form of several new songs written for him by Harry Lauder's own ballad writer, J. Hall Nicol.

One such song that Walter had bought outright, "Flora," went thusly:

1. A nice wee lass is Flora
The Lass I'm coortin' noo,
A soorock frae the Hielans'
She's my Bonnie Cushie Doo.
Tae ramble through the heather
Wi' this lass I never tire.
I'll need tae jine the Fire Brigade,
She set my heart on fire.

Chorus:
My wee Scots Darlin,
Is Flora McIntyre,
A lump o' Hielan honey,
She's the lassie I admire,
Reared among the heather hills,
Her cheeks are like the rose,
Ye could hang yer Tam o'Shanter
On her wee pug nose.

2. I'll no forget the summer day,
I met this pretty maid,
We strolled amang the heather,
An' I rowed her in my plaid,
Says she tae me behave yersel,
Ye'll mak me rin awa,
Ye'd better see a barber,
Fer yer whiskers' like a saw.

3. Flora's goin' tae merry me,
She's fixed the day in Spring,
I've saved up one and sixpence,
For tae buy the wedding ring,
Tae drive us tae the minister,

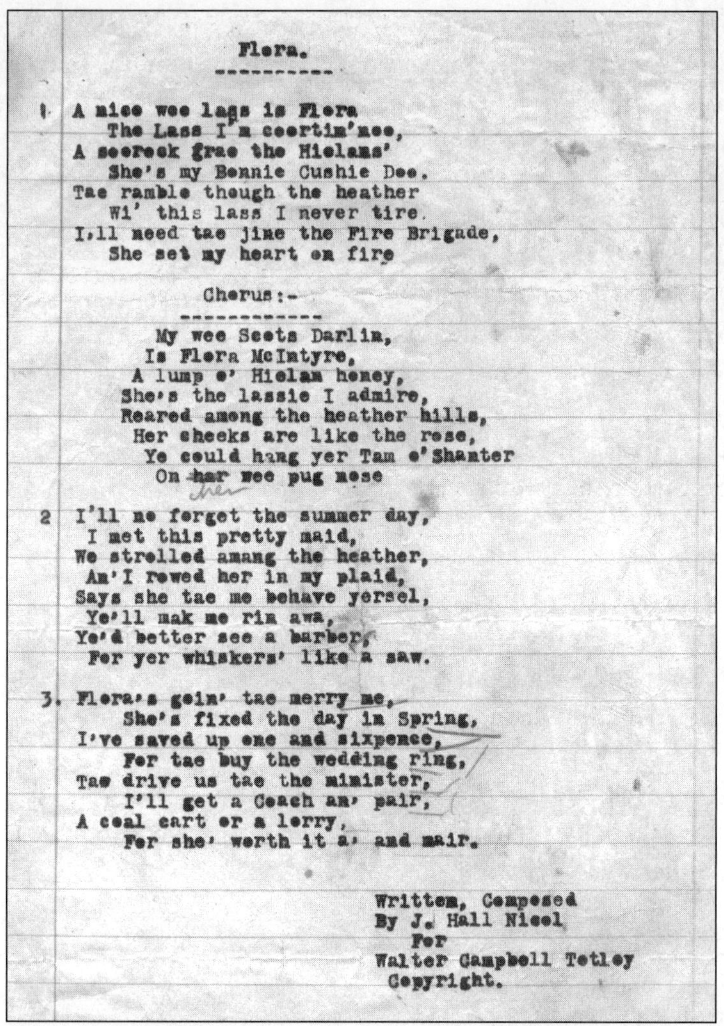

Flora.

1. A nice wee lass is Flora
   The Lass I'm coortin' noo,
A soorock frae the Hielans'
   She's my Bonnie Cushie Doo.
Tae ramble though the heather
   Wi' this lass I never tire.
I,ll need tae jine the Fire Brigade,
   She set my heart on fire

Chorus:-

My wee Scots Darlin,
Is Flora McIntyre,
A lump o' Hielan honey,
She's the lassie I admire,
Reared among the heather hills,
Her cheeks are like the rose,
Ye could hang yer Tam o'Shanter
On her wee pug nose

2 I'll ne forget the summer day,
 I met this pretty maid,
We strolled amang the heather,
 An' I rowed her in my plaid,
Says she tae me behave yersel,
 Ye'll mak me rin awa,
Ye'd better see a barber,
 For yer whiskers' like a saw.

3. Flora's goin' tae merry me,
   She's fixed the day in Spring,
I've saved up one and sixpence,
   For tae buy the wedding ring,
Tae drive us tae the minister,
   I'll get a Coach an' pair,
A coal cart or a lorry,
   For she' worth it a' and mair.

Written, Composed
By J. Hall Nicol
For
Walter Campbell Tetley
Copyright.

I'll get a Coach an' pair,
A coal cart or a lorry,
For she's worth it a' and mair.

He returned sporting a golf bag which was such a personal prize that he refused to let others carry it. He learned the game of golf on the wonderful rolling hills of Scotland during off days. Walter still found outdoor pursuits more to his liking, especially after being cooped up in studios and theatres. Growing a little older, a love of horseback riding, fishing and golf began to take the place of baseball and football in his heart.

In October of 1934 Walter began appearing more regularly on *Ameri-*

can School of the Air, as part of the "Hamilton Family" segment, playing one of the three sons who learned their geography lessons as they visited various locales.

The child/adolescent was expanding his resumé of credits with a rapidity that never really tapered off until he hit his main series, *The Great Gildersleeve*. He was one popular young man. During the mid-1930's one reviewer wrote of him: "At one rehearsal of an Eddie Cantor program, I recall seeing Tetley, not only winning plaudits from Cantor for the way he was handling his lines, but even walking off with another kid's part after the latter fluffed repeatedly." His dedication to perfection—and the old adage, "do a professional job, and you'll get asked back"—was the key to his success. It was even reported that Walter once cracked his kneecap just before a broadcast, and he still went on without faltering.

He reportedly appeared on Edgar Bergen's program, though that credit was not listed by his father. Also on *The Rudy Vallee Show* (WEAF, 8-9 p.m.) he supported Boris Karloff in a drama entitled "There's Always Joe Winters."

One newspaper stated in the mid or late 1930's that Walter was earning nearly $1,000 a month from his numerous broadcasts. Mainly due to the zealous nature of Walter's manager-mother who had hiked Walter's acting fees up 600%—because she could get it.

CHAPTER 6

After Walter had returned from his UK tour NBC announced in the fall of 1934 that their favorite little supporting player would finally have his chance at a lead. *Thrills of Tomorrow*, a 15-minute dramatic series for boys, was launched on Friday October 19th over the NBC-WEAF network at 6 p.m. E.S.T. The A.C. Gilbert company sponsored the show which visualized the part "inventions of today may play in the every day life of tomorrow." Walter played Spike Butler, "eager

Walter Tetley in the NBC series, Thrills of Tomorrow.

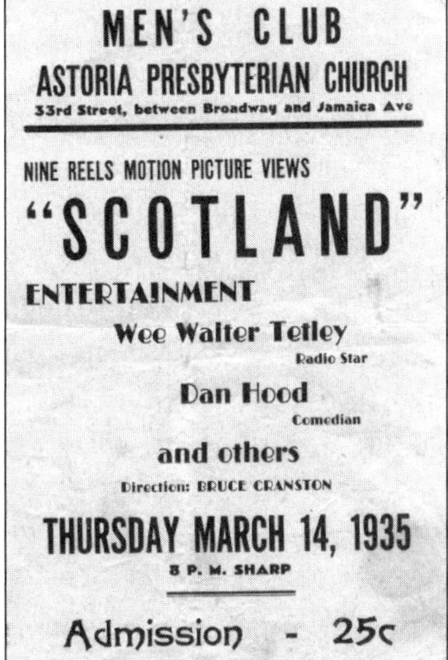

MEN'S CLUB
ASTORIA PRESBYTERIAN CHURCH
33rd Street, between Broadway and Jamaica Ave

NINE REELS MOTION PICTURE VIEWS
"SCOTLAND"

ENTERTAINMENT
Wee Walter Tetley
Radio Star
Dan Hood
Comedian
and others
Direction: BRUCE CRANSTON

THURSDAY MARCH 14, 1935
8 P. M. SHARP

Admission - 25c

and curious in dramas of seadromes, combination airplanes and dirigibles, recovery of gold from the ocean's floor and other exciting possibilities of the future. No fantastic or improbable feats will be presented in the series, and each broadcast will deal with a scientific venture regarded as feasible by recognized engineers."

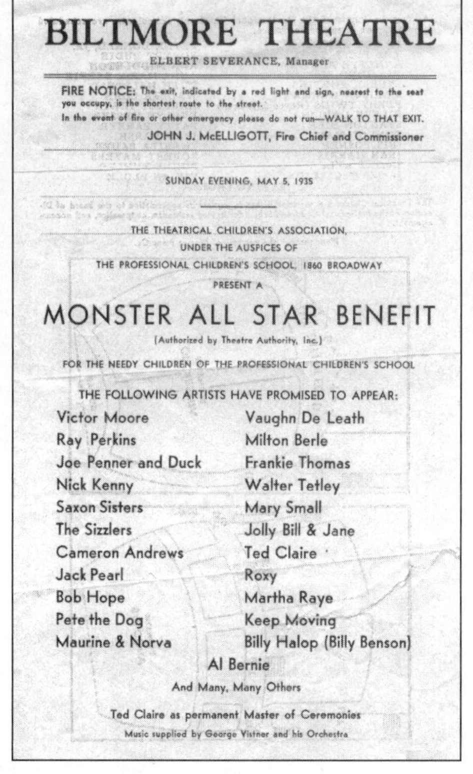

BILTMORE THEATRE

ELBERT SEVERANCE, Manager

FIRE NOTICE: The exit, indicated by a red light and sign, nearest to the seat you occupy, is the shortest route to the street.
In the event of fire or other emergency please do not run—WALK TO THAT EXIT.
JOHN J. McELLIGOTT, Fire Chief and Commissioner

SUNDAY EVENING, MAY 5, 1935

THE THEATRICAL CHILDREN'S ASSOCIATION,
UNDER THE AUSPICES OF
THE PROFESSIONAL CHILDREN'S SCHOOL, 1860 BROADWAY
PRESENT A

MONSTER ALL STAR BENEFIT

(Authorized by Theatre Authority, Inc.)

FOR THE NEEDY CHILDREN OF THE PROFESSIONAL CHILDREN'S SCHOOL

THE FOLLOWING ARTISTS HAVE PROMISED TO APPEAR:

Victor Moore — Vaughn De Leath
Ray Perkins — Milton Berle
Joe Penner and Duck — Frankie Thomas
Nick Kenny — Walter Tetley
Saxon Sisters — Mary Small
The Sizzlers — Jolly Bill & Jane
Cameron Andrews — Ted Claire
Jack Pearl — Roxy
Bob Hope — Martha Raye
Pete the Dog — Keep Moving
Maurine & Norva — Billy Halop (Billy Benson)
Al Bernie
And Many, Many Others

Ted Claire as permanent Master of Ceremonies
Music supplied by George Vistner and his Orchestra

Written by Raymond Scudder, the first episode dealt with "the possibilities of seadromes spaced at 500-mile intervals across the ocean." Spike Butler was joined in his adventuring by Pete Farley, played by Ned Weaver.

As 1935 came around, Walter's personal appearances were still going strong. At the Astoria Presbyterian Church on 33rd Street in New York City the Men's Club presented a "Scotland" night which of course had to include wee Walter Tetley, joined by comedian Dan Hood. Bruce Cranston directed the March 13, 1935 show which also included a 9-reel motion picture "view of Scotland." The performance began at 8 p.m. SHARP, admission was a quarter.

On a Sunday evening on May 5, 1935 Walter took part in one of the biggest celebrity charity shows of his career. The Monster All-Star Benefit, authorized by Theatre Authority, Inc., was presented by the Theatrical Children's Association, "under the auspices of the Professional Children's School" at 1860 Broadway in New York City, "for the needy children of the Professional Children's School." Ted Claire was the Master of Ceremonies leading a stellar cast including Victor Moore, Joe Penner and Duck, Jack Pearl, Bob Hope, Milton Berle, Billy Halop, Martha Raye and many others. Music was supplied by George Vistner and his orchestra.

Later that month the First Presbyterian Church of Edgewater, New

Jersey invited their Walter for a benefit concert given at the Eleanor Van Gelder School on May 23, 1935 at 8 p.m. It was a musical evening, with songs from xylophonist Yoichi Hiraoka, tenor Ernest Latowsky, and soprano Bertha Tanner Richards. Walter sang some of his regulars, plus a few new songs brought back from the UK. After a bagpipe solo he entertained the audience with "The Trousers That Me Father Used to Wear," "Whistle in the Thistle" and others.

CONCERT
FOR THE BENEFIT OF THE
FIRST PRESBYTERIAN CHURCH
Edgewater, New Jersey
AT THE ELEANOR VAN GELDER SCHOOL
MAY 23, 1935 at 8 P. M.

PROGRAM

My Lovely Celia .... Higgins
Rosalie .... DeKoven
Thank God for a Garden .... Del Riego
ERNEST LATOWSKY, Tenor
Florence Hubbart at the Piano

By the Beautiful Blue Danube .... Strauss—Schulz—Evler
MIRIAM SHIELDS, Pianist

Spring's Awakening .... Sanderson
BERTHA TANNER RICHARDS, Soprano
Ellmer Zoller at the Piano

Tanzerin von Sevilla .... Grunow
Ave Maria .... Schubert
Dance of the Goblins .... Bazzini
YOICHI HIRAOKA, Xylophonist
Miriam Shields at the Piano

She's the Lass for Me .... Lauder
Wiggle Waggle o' the Kilt .... Lauder
WALTER TETLEY, Juvenile Harry Lauder

To Sevilla .... Dessaner
Standchen .... Schubert
ERNEST LATOWSKY

Vo Mine Berge Muss i Scheide .... Swiss Folk-song
S'trotzig Dirndel .... Heinze
BERTHA TANNER RICHARDS, American Swiss Soprano

Bag-pipe Solo
The Trousers that ma Faither Used to Wear .... Mills
Whistle in the Thistle .... Burke
WALTER TETLEY

Andanti from "Surprise" Symphony .... Haydn
La Serenata .... Tosti
Second Hungarian Rhapsody .... Liszt
YOICHI HIRAOKA

Also that month a pleasant article appeared in *Radioland*, giving evidence to Walter's breadth and stamina: "Perhaps the most promising comedian of the future is a fourteen-year-old lad—Walter Tetley of *Buck Rogers* and *Bar X Days* fame, who has been a featured radio player for eight years. Walter is amazingly mature and workmanlike, switching from character to character with the ease and deftness of a Ted Bergman [later known as Alan Reed]. Watching him in a rehearsal of the Fred Allen show, of which cast he is a regular member, it was surprising to see him portray five different characters in three different dialects in the space of a half hour.

"From the Allen rehearsal he rushed to an adjoining studio where Miss Madge Tucker was putting her kids through their paces for the Sunday morning *Children's Hour*. She requested Walter to sing one of the songs he had brought back from Europe after an extensive tour through the British Isles, preferably one with patter in some dialect to serve as a setting for the number. Walter replied casually, 'I haven't one with patter, but I can *write some in*.' And write some in he did right there in the control room. Many a highly-paid comedian tearing his hair for new ideas and gags would have been proud to admit ownership to the Cockney monologue this fourteen-year-old prodigy dashed off so glibly."

On July 7, 1935 Walter was heard as guest artist on *Star Dust* over WAAT. He appeared in the Hotel Plaza ballroom dressed in kilt, carrying his bagpipes. He also performed an original comedy song, accompanied by Jay Stanley on the piano, in which he had to use eight different dialects, including his usual English, Cockney, French, Italian, German and Irish. And then he did a first for *Star Dust*: he played those bagpipes. After the performance he was besieged by fans and spent the next half hour signing autographs.

In early July he also began regular appearances on *The Simpson Boys*, "at Sprucehead Bay, in which he is heard as that incorrigible little rascal, Otie Bean." It was a weekly half-hour series on NBC starring Parker Fennelly and Arthur Allen. Early titles for the show were *Snow Village Sketches, The Stebbins Boys* and *Uncle Abe & David.*

The summer of this year saw busy Tetley racing from radio show to vaudeville house, playing all the theatres within commuting distance to New York so he would never have to miss a radio broadcast. His new stage act gave Walter the opportunity to sing in Scottish, Jewish and cockney dialects. He also began assisting his patter writer Arthur Behim in writing the material.

It was around the fall of '35 when Walter had to drop out of the seventh grade due to the grueling radio work that left him no time for personal appearances at his *own* high school. But a tutor had been hired to continue his education and get him ready for college. He excelled in French, causing his tutor to report that his ear for accents was so keen, he could have been a French instructor. The fact that Tetley was 20 years old in 1935 either meant the article that reported this fact was fed the wrong birth date (the most probable reason), or Mrs. Tetley kept Walter's true age a secret even from the school.

Walter was scheduled to appear at a Newark theatre in the fall, but his schedule was already full: *Buck Rogers* on Mondays, Tuesdays and Wednesdays at 6 p.m., and *Bobby Benson* on Mondays, Wednesdays and Fridays at 6:15 p.m. Somehow he managed to fill in the odd gaps with appearances on the shows of Joe Penner, Burns and Allen, Jack Benny and George Givot. *Buck Rogers* was his favorite program at the time, one of the reasons being that series author Jack Johnstone also did the sound effects on the show. Walter got a kick out of the electric shaver that was used to make the sound for the "noise from another world."

One thing that all newspaper reports agreed on at the time was that 15 (really 20) year old Walter had boundless energy. "Engaging, friendly and wholesome" were words found more often than not in the press, and all were deeply pleased at Walter's unaffected nature. For all his success, he remained unspoiled and the epitome of that little kid (minus the accents) he continued to play.

An article in the *Sullivan County Republican* related one reporter's sit in with Walter on an October 1935 episode of *Bobby Benson's Adventures*. He was amazed at the wealth these kids made and the busy lives they led at such a young age. "I wonder if their thousands of little listeners can believe that when Bobby (Billy Halop) says leisurely 'HO Oats for the kid who knows his oats' he has his hat and coat on and is half out the door in his haste to rush off, I assumed, to another child program elsewhere." Bobby, a good friend of Walter's at that time, had been on the air since he was 4 years old.

The reporter also spent time with Walter's mother who was only too eager to tell the press of her son's many radio credits. "I don't suppose she meant his salary to be published but I must admit I was floored when she told me what he earns in a week."

It was still profitable to be a "kid." On December 1st he proved that in yet another way by regularly appearing on *Funnies*, a weekly Sunday morning show on which comic strips were read over the air.

Chapter 7

In a 1936 interview, Walter stated, "I started in show business when I was five years old doing a single act in vaudeville. I was seven when my mother was working on a case as a registered nurse and the mother of the little girl she was taking care of knew that I was working. She suggested that I do some radio work and got me an audition with NBC. The next thing I knew I was singing Scottish songs on *The Children's Hour* over WJZ New York every Sunday morning."

It was due to his mother that Walter was now making well beyond the $100 a week he had been getting for his constant radio work. He owed his entire career to his mother who saw to it that his talent was always encouraged and showcased. Obviously Walter liked the show biz arena and publicly never had an unkind word to say against his determined mother, though she could ruffle feathers. Arthur Anderson wrote in his book *Let's Pretend*: "One of the best-organized and most aggressive stage mothers was Walter Tetley's. For years, until Walter finally moved to the West Coast, any director getting off the elevator on NBC's third floor knew that he would probably have to run a one-woman gauntlet with flaming red frizzy hair and steel-rimmed glasses consisting of Mrs. Tetley, who would accost him with, 'Don't you have anything for Walter today?'"

Even those who ordinarily didn't like working with kids found it hard to resist Walter's professionalism. Jack Johnstone, author of Walter's series *Buck Rogers* and later, *The Treasure Adventures of Jack Masters*, confessed his hatred of working with children, but singled out Walter as one of a kind.

Walter was also expertly complimented upon his performance in *The*

New Penny, starring Helen Hayes. In 1936 the actress' father wrote the star of *The New Penny* (Helen), suggesting that the show just wasn't worth listening to without Walter in it. That and a volume of other fan mail convinced the powers that be to write Walter back into the script quickly, with Walter as "Mickey" in a new storyline.

The New Penny was broadcast at 9:30 Tuesday nights on the Blue Network out of studio 3-E. Rehearsals were usually done on the preceding Monday between 3 and 4 p.m. Its sponsor was Sanka. Edith Meiser wrote the scripts, usually "knitting away on a sweater. But, every once in a while, without lifting her head, she adds some pertinent comment which is quickly noted by the artist referred to." (Miss Meiser also adapted the writings of Arthur Conan Doyle and wrote the radio scripts of detective Sherlock Holmes for radio during the 1930's and 1940's.) Joe Stauffer, a graduate of West Point, directed, and the announcer was Bill Adams. Tom McKnight, Mesier's manager, also functioned as production manager for the program, while the engineer was John Kulick. Around the end of December 1935 star Helen Hayes had refused an offer of $100,000 to do a film, preferring to stay with her series. "I place my home before any career," she said at the time. "Radio affords me the opportunity to remain near my family and yet be in the center of all theatrical activities—New York."

Part of the reason for the success of many child actors was due to the parental and ethical guidance he or she received. Mrs. Tetley was the family driving power, also businesswoman and schmoozer, even after little Walter had been firmly established. She would still accompany him to each of his broadcasts. Immediately upon entering the studio there would be an instant transformation from mother to business manager. However, always very professional in her attitude, she never went to an audition or rehearsal uninvited. She shrewdly observed:

"In my generation, children were raised to be seen and not heard. But that wouldn't be very good radio training for a child. So I have brought Walter up on the theory that parents should not be seen – or heard. I try never to put myself forward. Some of the stars who are very fond of Walter – Leslie Howard and Helen Hayes for instance – wouldn't even recognize me if they saw me."

She taught him how not to have an ego, and to always consider the audience's wishes before his own. He also never minded signing autographs after a performance. Though he would have much preferred to be off playing ping-pong with the studio page boys.

When something important cropped up, Tetley would be snatched from parties or holidays for an unscheduled broadcast or rehearsal. But the young man never complained. He loved the work.

In one of the few articles about him that did appear in a radio magazine, the little actor listed his ten do's and don'ts for being a success in radio:

1. Don't be late, for broadcasts or rehearsals.
2. Don't disappear after you get there. The director may have important notes. Don't get in his way either.
3. Know your part. Don't lose your script or your place.
4. Concentrate on the show—not sweets, nor the girls.
5. Do what you were hired for: reading lines, not playing the trombone.
6. Do what you're told, how you're told to do it. The director directs, the actor acts.
7. Dogs, roller skates and mothers must be kept out in the hall.
8. Don't ad lib unless you've been instructed to. Timing is everything.
9. Show your fans love, and respect. They control your present and future.
10. Don't act your age, but don't forget it! Don't call your elders by their first names, unless told otherwise.

He learned those rules through experience, and practiced them diligently. But when the show was over, Walter was a boy again. One press release suggested that he loved helping with hats and coats in the studio checkroom: his favorite pastime between broadcasts.

In his rare free time away from broadcasting studios he pursued his teenage interests. He always had a natural love of all competitive sports and once met his all-time idol Babe Ruth who gave him some baseball pointers. Besides his dogs, his other pets included seven turtles and a horse, or two. In 1936 the little radio star bought a 33-foot speedboat cabin cruiser. He invited a few of his radio co-stars to participate in the boat's christening. The scheduled event had to be postponed when it was found the date conflicted with the appearance of another great ship in the New

Walter and unknown friend taking the boat for a spin.

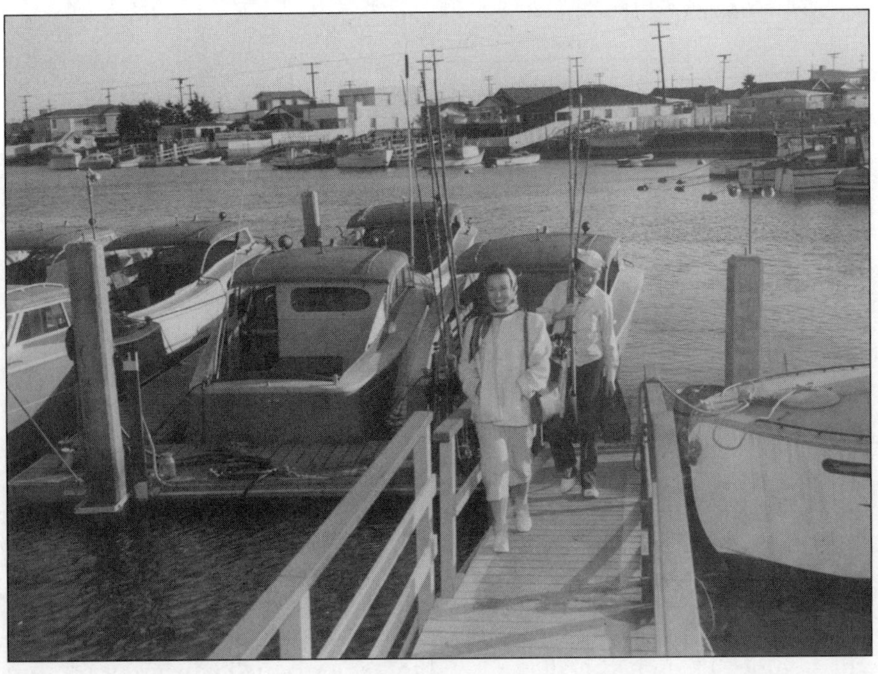

York harbor – *The Queen Mary*. When the christening took place, "Uncle Jim" Harkins from the *Town Hall Tonight* show was on hand, and actress Irene Rich did the honors, not with the usual bottle of champagne—but with a bottle of Welch's Grape Juice, the familiar, long-time sponsor of her radio show. NBC executives felt the event was worthy of broadcasting, and so it was.

Soon Walter was inviting friends over to cruise the New Jersey waterways. His friend and fellow actor Frank McIntyre, "Captain Henry" of *Show Boat*, was one of the first invited for a spin in the new craft. But the trip did not last long due to Captain Henry's bout with acute seasickness.

How Walter could be old enough to have a license for the craft and still be touted as a "kid" was unimportant and ignored.

He could afford the vessel, though. The "boy" was now bringing in $300 a week.

Around 1935/36 Walter was elected vice-president of an adult dramatic club in Edgewater, New Jersey, where he still lived. At his Roosevelt School, where he had won a five-dollar gold piece for being best speller, a song he wrote had been selected as Class Song.

In fact, the first five dollars Tetley ever received from a radio performance he gave to a fund to build President Roosevelt a swimming pool. He had real affection for Roosevelt, as Walter had had infantile paralysis when he was a baby. Sympathy for those in ill health was a trait that lasted Walter Tetley a lifetime. For years, ever since he was five years old, he performed in an annual show at the Crippled Children's Hospital in New York City. Nothing would make him break that date.

CHAPTER 8

As of 1935 Walter was still getting raves for his wee Sir Harry Lauder act. The *Albany Evening News* thought "his impersonation of a Scottish youngster on a recent Allen broadcast was magnificent. The burr was not overdone, as is generally the case. Indeed, all of this lad's efforts, so far as I'm concerned, are quite satisfactory. I think he ranks right up there with the best of the best…"

But by now he was getting a little tired of his Scottish act. He didn't want to be completely typecast as a dialect comedian. As an article at the time stated, "when he stepped into it six years ago, he was so well received on radio and stage that he didn't know it would grow irksome by the time he put on long pants and began to have aspirations to a stage career." If anything he was grateful for the plethora of work that was coming his way. To a kid who had to work through his childhood, who was never really allowed to grow up, all of the audio work allowed him a constant change of pace and character. He never grew bored.

On the contrary, there were some real perks to being NBC's number one "boy." He loved to go horseback riding. And what kind of kid would he be without a stab at offstage practical jokes? Tetley would buy tricks like an artificial fly he liked to wear on his coat lapel to lure the 'shoos' of his friends; not to mention running around with water pistols.

And as the dark days of the Depression crept on, his NBC salary crept up. $350 a week was rather good, regardless of the hours spent at his craft. Every Saturday night Mrs. Tetley would give her son $3.50 spending money, banking the rest and taking care of expenses. "He's remarkably talented," she admitted, "but that's no reason for letting too much money spoil him." There were a few times, though, when Walter managed "to fool mother. I save up for a couple of weeks and then I go on a real spree."

Though she served as his manager, she did it under the supervision of the National Broadcasting Company who managed his radio activities. Between Jessie and NBC, Walter was never without a new audition or public appearance to attend, formerly sanctioned by the radio company who always required credit in the billing.

Jessie would accompany her son to every broadcast he gave at Radio City. She would also see him on and off stage during his vaudeville appearances. In his dressing room between shows, there were lessons in French, English, Civics and Algebra to be studied with his tutor. At other times he engaged in correspondence courses. There was no free time to spend in classrooms.

"Sure, it's hard work," Walter admitted. "But I don't care, so long as I can be an actor. On the road, I don't care if I don't have regular meals, if the dressing rooms are cold or stuffy, or if I don't make a lot of money. But I've got to be an actor."

1936 was indeed a good year. Walter had been named Outstanding Child Actor in Radio for the previous year, and more series were lined up.

After several auditions for producer Hi Brown, on January 30, 1936 Tetley began appearing on *News of Youth*, a quarter-hour show broadcast on Monday, Wednesday and Friday from WABC's Studio #4 in New York City. The NBC series aired from 6:15 to 6:30 p.m. and was sponsored by the Ward Baking Company. The program held a solid cast of children and was produced by Hi Brown and Raymond Knight, the latter of which had produced *The Cuckoo Hour*.

Other 1936 series that began to crop up more frequently included *Death Valley Days*, a half-hour weekly drama about the old west; the hot crime drama, *Gang Busters*; *Renfrew of the Mounted*, AKA *Tales of the Canadian Mounted Police*, a half-hour series on CBS; *March of Time*, a weekly documentary-type show; *Old Dr. Jim*, a quarter-hour daily soap opera; and *The Treasure Adventures of Jack Masters*. He also showed up on episodes of *The Kate Smith Show, We the People, Home, Sweet, Home*, and at times (so it was reported) he substituted for Johnny, the calling pageboy for Phillip Morris cigarettes.

As of June 1936 Walter's "permanent address" was given as 5 Beverly Place, Edgewater, New Jersey. A promotional page taken out in *Billboard* showed his versatility by listing his various shows. The kid had a full week: *Paul Whiteman*, 9:30 p.m. Sundays; *Buck Rogers*, 6 p.m. Mondays, Wednesdays and Fridays; *Bobby Benson*, 6:15 p.m. Mondays, Wednesdays and Fridays; *Fred Allen* 9 p.m. Wednesdays; *Show Boat* 9 p.m. Thursdays. It was reported that he was making $700 a week and received a $3.50 weekly allowance.

CHAPTER 9

Throughout 1936 Tetley worked frequently with Fred Allen who greatly admired the little fellow's talents and had grown very fond of him. Whenever a script called for a "boy" voice, the wry comedian preferred Walter to any other young actor, commenting:

"Tet is a better actor than nine out of ten adults in radio, and he was just as good three years ago. That kid can do anything. The only reason he's not an English professor in Harvard right now is that radio pays better. When he plays my son in a skit, he mimics the voice perfectly in whatever accent I'm using. Chinese, Oxford, hillbilly, and he can do Scottish better than any of us.

"He bones up on his lines until he's letter perfect. He's actually got us in the habit of expecting so much from him that on a few occasions we've bawled him out for slight mistakes that we'd probably overlook in an adult. He cries like any sensitive kid does when you hurt his feelings, because of course he isn't the tough little brat he seems to be in some scripts—he wouldn't last fifteen minutes in this business if he was—and it's rather a shocking revelation after you've known him to discover he's just a child after all."

Walter suggested a few gags that worked their way into Wednesday night *Town Hall Tonight* broadcasts, and Allen urged the young man to write some sketches for the show. "But if I tried to do that," Walter said at the time, "I think I'd be overstepping myself."

Yet he was always proud of the show and being a part of the team called the Fred Allen Art Company: Minerva Pious, Lionel Stander, Eileen Douglas, Jack Smart, John Brown and Walter Tetley. Fred Allen himself would often bring Tetley copies of his press notices—good ones—for Walter's scrapbook. "They don't mean I'm good," Walter admitted, "they just mean my press agent is earning his salary."

One enthusiastic review of a specific episode gave it three stars. "The high spot of the first half was the skit with Fred, Portland, and that amazing boy actor who spouts polysyllables with all the ease of a radio editor splitting an infinitive."

But Walter was the kind of person who paid more attention to the rare bad notices, concerned about what went wrong or why the press was getting it wrong. One reviewed called Walter rather flippant, to which Tetley responded, "I don't like that. It will lead people to believe I think a lot of myself, and *that* isn't true."

Allen urged the ambitious youngster to try his luck in films, but his mother had some doubts if he could succeed in that visual medium.

Walter and his mother both felt that, now that he had been firmly established as a "well-known household voice," it would be advantageous for him to launch a career in motion pictures as well. So, after his usual morning appearance on *The Children's Hour*, the Tetleys began the long journey westward on Sunday, September 12, 1937.

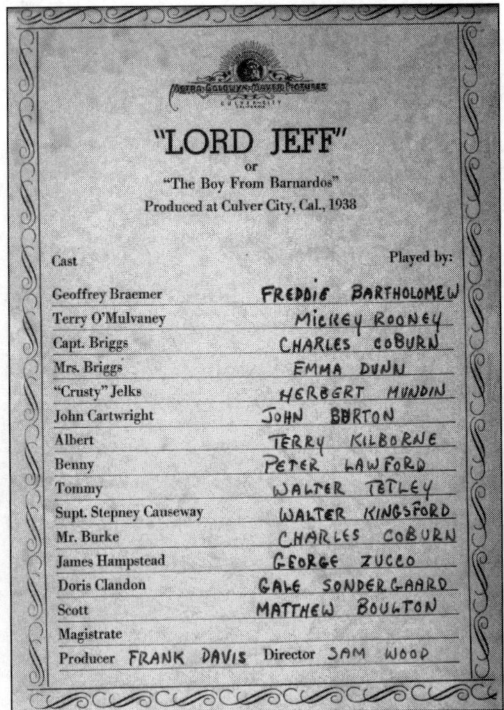

"LORD JEFF"
or
"The Boy From Barnardos"
Produced at Culver City, Cal., 1938

Cast	Played by:
Geoffrey Braemer	FREDDIE BARTHOLOMEW
Terry O'Mulvaney	MICKEY ROONEY
Capt. Briggs	CHARLES COBURN
Mrs. Briggs	EMMA DUNN
"Crusty" Jelks	HERBERT MUNDIN
John Cartwright	JOHN BURTON
Albert	TERRY KILBORNE
Benny	PETER LAWFORD
Tommy	WALTER TETLEY
Supt. Stepney Causeway	WALTER KINGSFORD
Mr. Burke	CHARLES COBURN
James Hampstead	GEORGE ZUCCO
Doris Clandon	GALE SONDERGAARD
Scott	MATTHEW BOULTON
Magistrate	

Producer FRANK DAVIS Director SAM WOOD

Certainly the move to Hollywood would bring continuing offers for work on network broadcasts. However, a profitable film career was never fully achieved. What few roles that came his way were mainly bits as bellhops and messenger boys. Still, during his short eight years (1938-1946) of work in motion pictures he was able to stack up credits for a number of significant films to add to his impressive resumé.

1938 was the start of his film career. He first appeared in *Sally, Irene and Mary* with

Prairie Moon , *Republic Pictures, 1938. Tommy Ryan, David Gorcey and Walter Tetley.*

The Spirit of Culver, *Universal Pictures, 1939.*

They Shall Have Music, *United Artists, 1939.*

later radio co-star Alice Faye. The film was set to open at Grauman's Chinese Theatre on March 4, 1938 at which time Miss Faye's and husband/co-star Tony Martin's feet were to be set in cement, but the event had to be postponed until March 20th since Alice fell ill.

The New Universal presents
JACKIE FREDDIE
COOPER · BARTHOLOMEW
in
"SPIRIT OF CULVER"
with
TIM HOLT · HENRY HULL · ANDY DEVINE · GENE REYNOLDS WALTER TETLEY · KATHRYN KANE · JACKIE MORAN
Original screenplay by Whitney Bolton and Nathanael West
Directed by JOSEPH SANTLEY
Associate Prod. BURT KELLY
1937

Walter had a brief part in *A Trip to Paris*, but it was the follow up feature at MGM that brought Walter one of his most prestigious films: *Lord Jeff,* AKA *The Boy from Barnardos*. The cast was a veritable Who's Who of Hollywood's young actors: Freddie Bartholomew, Mickey Rooney, Peter Lawford. Plus the big names of Charles Coburn, George

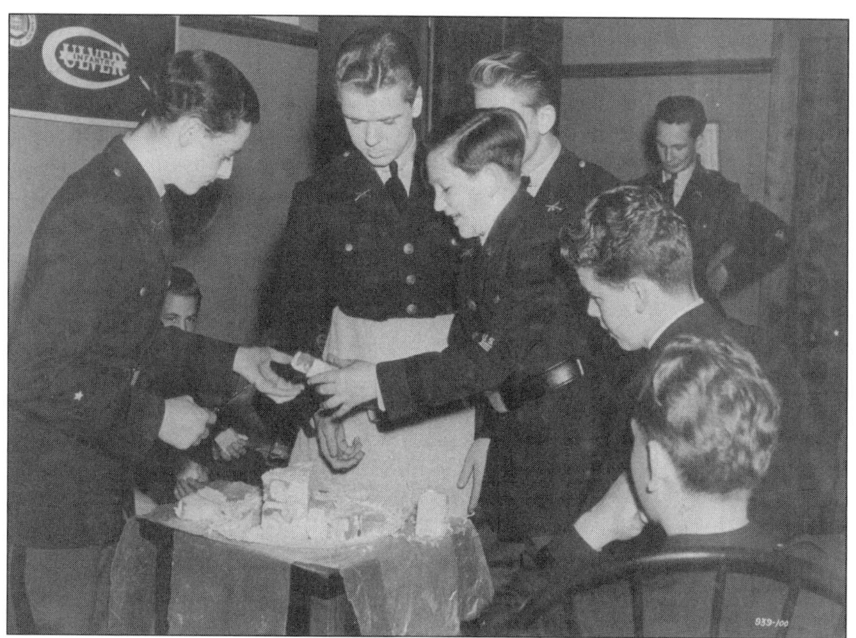

On the set of The Spirit of Culver *at Universal Studios. Cast members Freddie Bartholomew, Jackie Cooper, Jackie Moran, Gene Reynolds and Tim Holt help Walter celebrate his 23rd birthday. 1938.*

Boy Slaves, *RKO, 1939. Walter is leaning against the building.*

Let's Make Music, *RKO, 1941, with Elizabeth Risdon and Joyce Compton.*

Zucco, Gale Sondergaard and others. It was produced in Culver City, California by Frank Davis, with Sam Wood directing. Naturally, Tetley played a Scottish boy.

He then quickly reported to Republic Pictures for the part of the tough kid Mulligan in *Prairie Moon*, a western about three tough kids from Chicago who inherit a ranch when their father dies. The kids take their city ways out west, but Gene Autry sets them straight. After completion of the film Walter joined the cowboy star for some personal appearances.

In 1939 Walter made six films. He had a brief bit with W.C. Fields (the man who couldn't stand children) in *You Can't Cheat an Honest Man*. He was seen in *They Shall Have Music*, the story of an underprivileged young boy who wants to become a violin virtuoso. Walter had a wonderful scene in which he tried to exchange banjo lessons with famed violinist Yascha Heifitz for violin lessons. He also joined Boris Karloff as a chimney sweep in *The Tower of London*, one of many roles for which he received no screen credit.

Around 1939 a local paper from Tetley's own Bergen County in New Jersey proudly proclaimed "Walter Tetley is doing better than alright in Hollywood and he is not one of those blond effeminate screen lover types.

He is famous for his voice. For the past three weeks he has been providing the voice for the title role in Disney's *Pinocchio*." In fact, he had only made a voice test for the role.

With an even larger salary from film and radio work, Walter was now living in a more spacious home at 744 North Gramercy Place in Hollywood. It was there that he received a telegram of thanks on March 9, 1939 from Walter Wanger, chairman of the Hollywood branch of the Los Angeles Jewish Community Committee for his part in a radio program on the previous Monday night.

In that same year he appeared with Jackie Cooper, Freddie Bartholomew and Andy Devine in *Spirit of Culver*, directed by Joseph Santley, original screenplay by Whitney Bolton and Nathanael West. There was a rumor, printed in *National Box Office Digest* on February 17, 1939 that studio executives had delayed the film's premiere in order to preview the retakes that had been made in order to beef up Walter's part. He played "Rocks," the comic role. During the filming at Universal Walter tried to organize a Scottish bagpipe band among the youngsters on the lot, in order to join Jackie Cooper's band in a concert. If he was ever able to gather up enough eclectic talent is open to speculation.

Boy Slaves, *RKO, 1939.*

That was also the year 23-year-old Tetley played "Pee Wee" with Charles Powers, Johnny Fitzgerald and Anne Shirley in RKO's *Boy Slaves*. It was the powerful story of a group of kids who are besieged in a farmhouse and are threatened with killing by the brutal overseers of a turpentine camp from which they had escaped. The film was an impressive exposé of the harsh exploitation of child labor in the early part of the 20th century.

Meantime, Walter was still doing live shows in his Scottish persona. On June 15, 1939 a Police Benefit show in Rialto, California featured him in a production led by Frank Corbett in which "Pop-Eye the Sailor Man will appear at this performance with his company of actors." Other "leading Broadway vaudeville acts" appeared "through the courtesy of the Arthur Fisher Agency," including Uncle Don of radio fame, and the Wonder Dog! The musical director was Paul Scholz of Leo Feist Music Publishers, with music for the acts and dancing by Bob Oakley and band. A complete "picture show" was also part of the festivities, as well as prizes: the lucky boy received a baseball autographed by Babe Ruth and the lucky girl winner was presented with a Shirley Temple doll.

During 1940 Walter appeared in six films, two of which were uncredited. In *Emergency Squad*, directed by Edward Dmytryk, he played Matt. He was also in *Framed*, which had to do with a young newspaper reporter who finds himself framed for murder. It starred Frank Albertson and Constance Moore. Walter was cast as Cadet Blackburn in *Military Academy* which starred Tommy Kelly and *Dead End* star Bobby Jordan. In *Under Texas Skies* he portrayed the tough kid Theodore who was forced into having his hair cut in one short comic relief scene in this western starring Robert Livingston and Bob Steele. In *The Villain Still Pursued Her* Walter was cast as yet another (telegram) delivery boy in this Buster Keaton sound feature. And in the musical *Let's Make Music*, Tetley, as Eddie the office boy, joined an eminent cast of Bob Crosby, Jean Rogers, Joyce Compton, Benny Rubin and more.

CHAPTER 10

After a succession of bit parts in mostly minor films, Walter was ready for something more: a greater challenge, and more stability of work. When his life-changing radio series, *The Great Gildersleeve* came along, little Tetley was all set.

It was on *The Great Gildersleeve* that Walter achieved his greatest success. Hal Peary's Gildersleeve character had been popular enough on *Fibber McGee and Molly* to mark it as radio's first spin-off series. After an audition show made for the Johnson Company (Fibber's sponsor) on May 14, 1941, the series premiered for Kraft Foods on August 31, 1941. Gildersleeve, affectionately shortened to 'Gildy' by one of the main characters, was a middle-aged windbag who loved to boast as much as he loved to sing. Amidst romancing the local southern belle and locking horns with Judge Hooker, Gildy found his time in Summerfield filled up with taking care of his orphaned niece, Marjorie, and nephew, Leroy, played by Walter Tetley.

Gildy and Leroy.

Perennially-12-year-old Leroy was Walter's favorite role of his career.

It wasn't long before his catchphrases—"What a character!" "Are you kiddin'?" and "For corn's sake!"—were mimicked by his thousands of fans that wrote in weekly. Though Walter was at his most visible during the Gildy years, he still shied away from most personal publicity. He relished in using his new-found mega-stardom to help the many causes he still endowed with money or personal appearances. Nevertheless his private life was still kept strictly private.

Leroy was a positive role model for kids. He was the epitome of the ordinary boy who got into scrapes, let himself be talked into wild schemes for the sake of fun or money, but never gave his "Uncle Mort" (often just "Unk") any real, long-lasting trouble. The most exasperating "abuse" Gildy had to take was the constant deflating of the super ego, when Leroy would remind him of the truth behind his boasts.

A mature, long-legged Walter relaxes at home.

In 1976 Hal Peary recalled that a few years before the start of *Gildersleeve*, "Walter grew several inches after some treatment by a noted urologist here. I believe he was 22 at the time." Willard Waterman also remembered: "Walter's voice never changed, so he was able to play youngsters all of his life. He was about 5' 3" and had no facial hair, and his body was a little out of proportion. Nobody could get more out of a line than Walter." After the injections, Tetley shot up to around six feet tall.

Once Walter came on board the Gildersleeve series, his radio work ceased to be as prolific as it once was. Perhaps NBC wanted Tetley to be more associated with the Leroy role than anything else. Luckily the new-found fame led to roles, albeit small ones still, in more prominent films. In 1941 Walter's unmistakable voice was heard on the soundtrack of the Warner Brothers animated Looney Tunes cartoon, *The Haunted Mouse*. In 1942 he held tiny roles in features such as *Eyes in the Night*, the entertaining mystery about a blind private detective with Edward Arnold in the lead. And *Thunder Birds*, a World War II movie that dealt with flight training at Thunderbird Field, Arizona. He was a mere messenger boy in that, but 1942 was also the year of Tetley's biggest, and funniest role in a

A Yank at Eaton, *MGM, 1942.*

The Family Next Door, *Universal, 1939.*

Bud Abbott, Walter Tetley and Lou Costello in Who Done It?, *Universal Studios, 1942.*

film.

In the Abbott and Costello vehicle *Who Done It?* Walter was only slated for a small part in one scene. But Lou Costello knew a good supporting player when he saw one, and kept requesting new scenes to be added for him. It was probably Tetley's largest screen role, and he was a part of some of the best gags in the picture.

The film involved soda jerks (Bud and Lou) who really wanted to be radio writers: their own mystery series would star them as Muck and Mire. When the pair pose as detectives after a murder is committed, Abbott and Costello find themselves chased not only by the coppers, but by the killer as well (for a missing clue—a glove—that Costello had found).

It was a wartime plot which put Bud and Lou's pratfall and verbal comedy talents to perfect use. It also used Tetley's comic skills better than anything else outside of radio. One of the best gags was the counter scene in which the page boy (Tetley) boastfully bet the soda jerk (Costello) a nickel that he could drink a tall glass of orange juice faster than he could make it. The dopey soda jerk gleefully took the challenge, but he was the loser in the deal because he only collected one nickel for a half-dollar's worth of orange juice. It was a hilarious scene that required ten takes. Ironically, Walter was allergic to citrus juices.

The scheming page got the best of Costello throughout the film. In another scene when the comedian was extremely anxious to get into a radio broadcast, the crafty page informed him that he had some tickets that he could let him have—for a fee. After paying for the tickets, the page pocketed the money and then calmly said, "Oh, by the way—those tickets are for yesterday's broadcast." In disgust Costello tossed the tickets away. Whereupon the page picked them up, winked slyly and escorted several of his young lady friends into the broadcast.

Another "cameo" came in *Pride of the Yankees*, the hit sentimental Gary Cooper baseball film. One reviewer wrote: "clever fictionalizing and underplaying of the actual sport in contrast to the more human, domestic side of the great ballplayer make the film good box-office for all audiences, not forgetting the femmes." Tetley was seen as the uncredited cake delivery boy.

Walter was in good company for *Invisible Agent*, a 1942 wartime entry in the Universal horror series started by Claude Reins as the see-through villain in the original 1933 *Invisible Man*. This time, Jon Hall is Frank Raymond, grandson of that original inventor, who is dropped into Germany to gather information from the bewildered Nazi leaders, played by arch-villains Peter Lorre and Sir Cedric Harwicke. It was a good war propaganda film to cheer for; unfortunately, Walter was again used in merely a small walk-on role.

In 1942's *Gorilla Man* Walter was in the film enough for his character to have a name. He was Sammy. The incredible wartime plot involves Captain Craig Killian, played by John Loder, returning from a Continental raid with his British commandos. He has vital information, but is steered by Nazis to their private sanitarium so they can prevent him delivering the information. They discredit him with a few murders, but of course in the end he manages to round up the gang.

Typical of Hollywood, when *The Great Gildersleeve* had its chance to shine as a film series, almost all of the elements—particularly the cast—which made the radio show such a success were completely recast. The only exceptions were Harold Peary as Gildy and Lillian Randolph as Birdie. Margie was now played by Nancy Gates, and little Leroy had a real kid in the role for a change: Freddie Mercer.

The first film of the series, *The Great Gildersleeve*, received the most praise. Though the film was sorely lacking its Tetley support, *Variety* didn't seem to mind all of the substitutions. "Nancy Gates, a youngster, and Freddie Mercer, a ten-year-old lad, as Margie and Leroy, familiar characters of the radio shows, are neatly cast." It was released on January 2, 1943.

The series was followed by *Gildersleeve on Broadway, Gildersleeve's Bad Day*, and *Gildersleeve's Ghost*, all with Freddie Mercer featured in the Leroy role. Tetley did manage a bit part as a bellhop in *Gildersleeve on Broadway* in 1943. *Variety* couldn't stand the film, calling the story "a shoddy affair which bounces through a maze of stupid situations that are laughed *at* – rather than *with*."

But that was also the year Walter began lending his voice to Andy Panda cartoon shorts, as the lead character. The Walter Lantz creation began in 1939 for Universal Studios as a childlike, baby bear-type character. *Fish Fry*, Tetley's first of the series, was directed by Shamus Culhane. The plot involved Andy Panda buying a pet goldfish and trying to get it home before a hungry alley cat could do away with it. It was a cute character, and the seven-minute film was Oscar nominated for Best Short Subject. More Andy Panda cartoons followed through the 1940s, and were later repackaged for television in *The Woody Woodpecker Show* in 1957.

Tetley's dramatic abilities brought him roles on many different programs including such prestigious series as *Suspense*. On December 13, 1943 he supported Cary Grant on an episode entitled "The Black Curtain"; on April 27, 1944 he returned with Gene Kelly in "Death Went Along for the Ride"; on November 16, 1944 with Robert Cummings in "Dead of Night"; on February 8, 1945 with Claire Trevor and Nancy Kelly in "Tale of Two Sisters"; and on August 8, 1946 he was heard with Cathy and Elliot Lewis in "Dead Ernest."

In February of 1947 he was heard in a supporting role on *The Alan Young Show*. Also in 1947 the Mutual Network began an anthology series, *Family Theater*, at the suggestion of a Catholic priest, Father Patrick Peyton, in an effort to promote family unity and prayer. Each week varying guest stars donated their services free of charge. Walter appeared a number of times. On July 24, 1947 he was heard on the episode entitled "Brass Buttons," about a tough policeman, and on January 8, 1948 he returned in "The Happiest Person in the World" with William Bendix and Bea Benaderet. The role gave him a rare chance to display his many talents.

During 1944 he had a number of varying film roles. In *Bowery to Broadway* he had a brief bit, and appeared as a grocery delivery boy in *Molly and Me*, as well as a young soldier in *Follow the Boys*. Though the films were good and somewhat high profile, with his roles being so thankless and miniscule, it was no wonder Walter was getting fed up with his "movie career." He preferred radio, and with good reason.

When *The Great Gildersleeve* series was at its height of popularity, Walter was receiving a lot of fan mail. So was "Leroy." The "brat" once received a package containing the Van Court Scientific Course in Boxing to protect himself from his overbearing uncle, so believable was Tetley's performance.

During the series Walter lived with his family fifteen minutes out of Hollywood in the San Fernando Valley. There, at the place they named "Big Oak Ranch," they had room for their small farm and stable with two horses, one of which pulled an old-fashioned "surrey with the fringe on top" (and had been used in many films). Also around the spread could be found four dogs, five cats, two hundred chickens and two very unglamorous ducks which he whimsically named Hedy and Lana.

The home itself was an attractive white stucco Spanish-style house built around a big oak tree "whose branches afford a natural cooling system." It was Walter's haven away from the rush of Hollywood work, where he could lounge around his swimming pool with his father who seemed to spend all his time there. His mother was then a Lieutenant Colonel in the Women's Emergency Corps and was in charge of a free canteen for servicemen in Beverly Hills. His brother was a precision parts inspector in a nearby defense plant.

Chapter 11

Though Walter appeared in six films in 1944, his movie career was clearly winding down. He played a small bit as a call boy in the Jack the Ripper thriller, *The Lodger*, starring Laird Cregar, George Sanders and Merle Oberon. Also, he had a bit part in *Her Primitive Man* with Louise Allbritton. He could be seen briefly as the florist's assistant in *Casanova Brown*, starring Gary Cooper.

He appeared as an uncredited messenger (again) in *Pin Up Girl*, a Technicolor musical with plenty of splash and lots of Betty Grable. *Variety* said, "This is one of those escapist film musicals which you accept, or else. It makes no pretences at ultra realism, and if you get into the mood fast, it's something to occupy your attention for an hour and a half. It's all very pleasing and pleasant." Joe E. Brown and Martha Raye provided the comic support, while songsters Mark Gordon and James Monaco supplied some catchy tunes.

Being cast in very minor parts in highly popular films left the young actor feeling ungratified.

The year 1945 didn't bring much in the way of film roles. His old friend Fred Allen offered him a walk-on role in *It's in the Bag*. Walter's cameo appearance was just one of many that dotted this revue-type movie. Others of the old Allen's Alley members were also seen briefly. The plot was a mish-mosh of zany antics by Allen, who inherited a load of cash, which had been sewn inside the lining of one of a set of matching chairs. But they had been scattered hither and yon. One chair was in Jack Benny's apartment, and another was found in a crowded restaurant featuring a trio of singing waiters made up of Rudy Vallee, Don Ameche and Victor Moore.

Although Allen's fans found it a "rather delightful collection of comedy pearls strung together," doleful critics weren't amused. A review in *Variety* stated: "this rat's nest of nonsense defies the sober description of a rational mind…" Be what may, it is unfortunate that Tetley was given almost nothing to do.

His final screen appearance was with comedian Bert Gordon (father of actor/singer Barry Gordon), who is best remembered by radio listeners as "the Mad Russian" on the Eddie Cantor program. The title of the film was also Gordon's catchphrase, *How Do You Do?* It did not do very well at the box office.

After supplying the voice in a few more Andy Panda animated cartoons, Tetley gave up films in favor of his more substantial radio work.

In 1947 he was signed for a leading role in a syndicated, transcribed domestic comedy, *The Anderson Family*. Doing the recordings supplied further steady employment.

Then in 1948 it finally appeared that Walter's "big break" was about to take place. NBC announced plans to star him in a series of his own to be entitled, *The Kid on the Corner*. The comedy would revolve around a wise-cracking corner newsboy during a newspaper "price war." A script was prepared, and Sheldon Leonard was cast in a supporting role. An audition recording was made on April 10, 1948. All went well, the audi-

Tetley and friends at The Cocoanut Grove club in Los Angeles

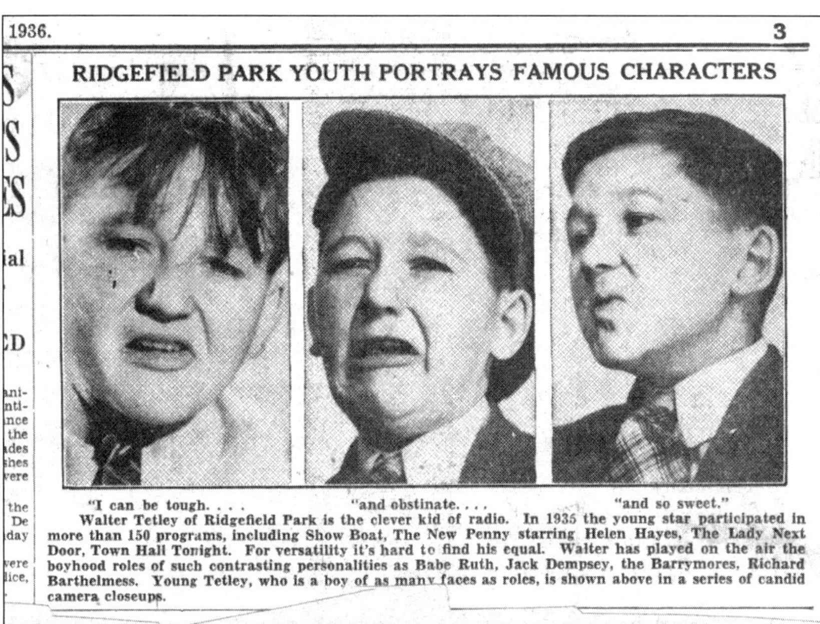

1936. 3

RIDGEFIELD PARK YOUTH PORTRAYS FAMOUS CHARACTERS

"I can be tough. . . . "and obstinate. . . . "and so sweet."

Walter Tetley of Ridgefield Park is the clever kid of radio. In 1935 the young star participated in more than 150 programs, including Show Boat, The New Penny starring Helen Hayes, The Lady Next Door, Town Hall Tonight. For versatility it's hard to find his equal. Walter has played on the air the boyhood roles of such contrasting personalities as Babe Ruth, Jack Dempsey, the Barrymores, Richard Barthelmess. Young Tetley, who is a boy of as many faces as roles, is shown above in a series of candid camera closeups.

Walter Tetley, prince of brat voices.

Walter (looking a little self-conscious) with his friends Mrs. and Mr. Wade, Jessie Campbell Tetley and her sister Anna Campbell, at a wedding reception.

Walter with friends: Mr. and Mrs. Wade, Edward Everett Horton and Wallace Ford.

ence reacted favorably, and it looked good, but for unknown reasons the network decided against picking up the show. Another in a never-ending string of heartbreaking disappointments.

It may have been a relief at the time. Starring in a series would bring many more added responsibilities, plus much more public attention, endless interviews and much less privacy. Walter had become very set in his ways. He did not want the spotlight constantly focused upon him. He was the sort who enjoyed his work, but when the microphone was turned off and the applause died down, he preferred to leave it all behind, and simply "go home." This same attitude may have made it easier when he eventually left the business.

But in 1948 – October 3rd to be exact – Walter began his second most famous role: that of the insufferable, loud mouth delivery boy, Julius Abbruzio on *The Phil Harris/Alice Faye Show*. Sporting a semi-Brooklyn accent, Julius was almost the exact opposite of the good-natured Leroy. The impish lad delighted in causing trouble, playing jokes and generally giving Phil and Remley a hard time.

Bowling with Alice Faye and friends.

The Harris-Faye series was rather a spin-off *of The Jack Benny Program*, with Phil and Alice playing themselves, taking the character Frankie Remley (noted for being drunk all the time on Jack's show) into their world. Many of the plots were like *The Flintstones/Honeymooners*, involving Phil and Frankie's wild exploits. Rexall Drugs sponsored the show which cost $14,500 a week to produce.

Walter usually emerged in the second half of the half-hour program, when the boys were already in hot water. Julius had a few cute catch phrases to shout back at them: a Leroy-type "Are you kiddin'?" and the more New York-oriented "Get outta here!" The audience ate it up.

It must have felt like old home week when Fred Allen visited the January 23, 1949 program. Though Walter had no scenes with Fred, the two traded stories and caught up on old times before and after the show. The following excerpt from that episode is typical of Tetley's role in the fun. Julius would start out as a wise guy, relishing in taunting Harris and Remley about whatever they were getting themselves into that week. But as the comedy increased, the worm, and tables, slowly turned on the poor little delivery boy:

HARRIS: It's no use, Frankie, this suit of Willie's doesn't fit me.

FRANKIE: I don't know. You got it on, didn't you?

HARRIS: Just barely. It's too tight. Look at the way these pants cling to my legs. How does it look, Remley?

FRANKIE: Very alluring. It looks like black underwear.

HARRIS: Well, I don't care how it looks. I got my heart set on that Ball and I'm going. And now that we found Willie's invitation you can go too.

FRANKIE: Yeah, I—(TAKE) Hey, wait a minute. I just happened to think, I haven't got a full dress suit either.

HARRIS: Where can we get one for you?

FRANKIE: I don't know, but I'll get one if I have to go through every transom in this hotel.

SOUND: DOOR OPENS

FRANKIE: Come on. Curly, I'm in a hurry, move faster.

HARRIS: I can't. This dress suit of Willie's is choking me, all over. If I make a sudden move I'll split it.

FRANKIE: Well, stop waddling. You look ridicu…

TETLEY: Hiya, Mr. Remley, I…Hey, Mr. Remley, where you going with that penguin?

HARRIS: I ain't no penguin, Julius.

TELTEY: Oh it's Mr. Harris. What are you made up for?

HARRIS: I'm going to the President's Ball and this is my full dress suit.

TETLEY: This is a full dress suit?

HARRIS: Yeah. How do I look, kid?

TETLEY: (LAUGHS) Oh brudder are you bow legged.

FRANKIE: Curly ain't bow legged. He just happens to have a well-turned ankle, all the way up to the knee.

HARRIS: Well, maybe I'm a *little* bow legged.

TETLEY: A *little*? You look like you're standing on a pair of ice tongs.

HARRIS: You got a lot of nerve making fun of me. You look a little baggy yourself. What have you got on under that overcoat?

TETLEY: My full dress suit. My Uncle Herman got me an invitation to the Ball.

FRANKIE: You're wearing a full dress suit?—Curly, what do you think?

HARRIS: It's a little short but if you walk on your knees I think you can make it.

FRANKIE: Right. Julius, stand still.

TETLEY: Hey you guys, quit measuring me.

FRANKIE: Hold still. Think we can get away with this, Curly?

HARRIS: (SING SONG) We can try.

FRANKIE: (SING SONG) Let's get started.

TETLEY: (SING SONG) Over my dead body...Oh, oh, I shouldn't have said that.

HARRIS: Grab him, Frankie!

FRANKIE: Got him!

TETLEY: Get your paws offa me, you guys!

HARRIS: Quiet! A little slow music Remley, while I disrobe him. (FRANKIE SINGS "A PRETTY GIRL")

TETLEY: (YELLS) Stop taking my coat off. Let go of me! Gimme back my pants! Help! Help! Clothes-nappers!

Most often Julius would get the better of Phil and his chum:

JULIUS: When you left town I didn't think they'd let you back in this country.

PHIL: Why?

JULIUS: Because it's against the law to smuggle dope across the border.

The beloved series ran through June 18, 1954.

Chapter 12

At some point Walter appeared briefly with an all-star radio cast on the 3-album set, *A Christmas Carol*, for Columbia Records.

Scrooge:	Basil Rathbone
Fred:	Elliott Lewis
Bob Cratchet:	Jay Novello
Marley's Ghost:	Arthur Q. Bryan
Christmas Past:	Francis X. Bushman
Scrooge as a Boy:	Tommy Cook
Little Fan:	Rhoda Williams
Christmas Present:	Stuart Robertson
Mrs. Cratchet:	Paula Winslowe
Peter:	Dix Davis
Martha:	Lurene Tuttle
Tiny Tim:	Tommy Cook
1st Man:	Arthur Q. Bryan
2nd Man:	Stuart Robertson
Charwoman:	Paula Winslowe
Undertaker's Man:	Raymond Lawrence
Boy:	Walter Tetley
Narrator:	Harlow Wilcox

Between two hit series, an occasional guest shot and personal appearances, Walter showed no signs of slowing down, even though radio's days were numbered. On October 18, 1949 Walter made one of his rare television appearances, as guest on Joe Graydon's show over KLAC-TV at 9:30 p.m. Three days later Tetley called the square dance given at the Woodland Hills Community Center. He stomped his foot to the fiddle from 8 to 11 p.m. and had a ball, especially since he knew the event benefited the newly opened Woodland Hills Co-operative Nursery. Again, he gave his services freely. According to other accounts, it wasn't the first or last time he led that square dance.

Both of Walter's radio series had a featured spot in the Santa Claus Lane Parade of Stars in Hollywood on November 16, 1949. It was led by the Phil Harris family, with the cast of *The Great Gildersleeve*, including Hal Peary, Marylee Robb and Walter, following later.

As of Christmas Eve of that year Walter was a civic leader in San Fernando Valley, belonged to the Chamber of Commerce, was a member of the San Fernando Valley Boy Scouts' executive council, was associate Scout Master for a troop of handicapped boys (Rainbow Troop #1260), and was honorary president of the Metropolitan Soccer League.

On January 25, 1950 Phil Harris and the entire cast headed to New York to begin work on the March of Dimes campaign. They taped their January 29, February 5 and 12 shows from New York, and headed back to California for the February 19 program.

The *Citizen News* from Hollywood reported on February 24, 1950 that starting on March 25th Walter would be conducting "a dramatic school in his barn." Two days later he was very saddened to learn of the death of his idol, Sir Harry Lauder, at the age of 80.

An older and wiser Walter Tetley.

In a way, Walter Tetley's show-biz career ended with radio's end. *The Great Gildersleeve* ended its long, prestigious run on March 21, 1957, finally losing the long battle against television. Many of radio's top voices either migrated to television or cartoon work. Walter did too, to a limited extent.

In 1956 he was hired by UPA

to supply a voice in the *Gerald McBoing-Boing* TV series, in episodes of *Dusty of the Circus*. The series was later syndicated as part of *Mister Magoo and Friends*. Bill Scott, later of Bullwinkle fame (voicing Peabody to Walter's Sherman), was assistant producer on the show.

During the months of July through October 1957 Walter was heard briefly on *The Stan Freberg Show*, a summer replacement show for Jack Benny, and the last network comedy series of radio. Four years later Freberg underused Tetley again on his classic comedy album, *Stan Freberg Presents the United States of America Vol. 1*. Walter had a few lines in the Midnight Ride of Paul Revere and the discovery of electricity sketches.

It must have been hard for a workhouse like Tetley to adapt to a sudden loss of definite, incessant employment. It was not a happy time. According to Hal Peary, Walter's parents and the brother he lived with passed away sometime in the 1950s. Edward Everett Horton, another famous voice from *Rocky and Bullwinkle*, lived nearby. But it's difficult to say if he had any close friends to which he could confide his troubles.

Around this time Walter was presented with an award from the Hollywood Coordinating Council "for his outstanding personal service to handicapped and underprivileged children," mainly for organizing Boy Scout Troop 1260. This troop was comprised entirely of shut-ins who were unable to participate in regular scouting activities. He began a local radio program aimed at his Scouts so they could "meet" right in the homes of the boys who otherwise could not get out. He would also invite the Boy Scouts to his ranch in the San Fernando Valley where they would lounge around the pool, play with his prize-winning cocker spaniels and enjoy a home away from home.

Whether or not Walter had been a Boy Scout himself is open to question. It's doubtful that he had had the time for such normal activities in his youth, since his mother took him from one radio or public appearance to another *constantly*. Perhaps in later life, free from the push of his mother, he felt he could give other boys, who also never had a chance at an "ordinary" life, what he had always missed.

As the Gildersleeve and Phil Harris programs came to an end in the 1950s, Walter had more time on his hands than in previous years. He began to take refuge in an extra business pursuit, running a pet shop called The Happy Tail on Ventura Boulevard, inspired by his great interest and love of dogs. When the shop originated, or how long it continued, is uncertain.

Pantomime Quiz, *with Jimmy Lydon, Walter Tetley, Keefe Brasselle, Beverly Tyler, Mike Stokey (host, with fish), Adele Jergens, Hans Conreid, Robert Stack and Frank DeVol. Early 1950s.*

One of Tetley's few live television appearances came between 1949 and 1952 on *Pantomime Quiz*, which began as a local show in Los Angeles in 1948. The game show consisted of two teams of four celebrities each playing charades (subjects suggested by the viewers at home), guessing a famous phrase, quote, title, etc. within the two-minute time limit.

Hal Peary and Walter last worked together at a special Radio Night produced by Frank DeVol at the Hollywood Bowl in 1966. According to Peary, Walter "wow'd 'em as 'Leroy' and he had grown to nearly six feet at that time. Rather amazing! Walter's personal voice did change through the years but to quote him: 'I can still do Leroy. All I have to do is raise my eyebrows.'"

Chapter 13

Perhaps Walter's most enduring vocal performance was that of Sherman, Mr. Peabody's "pet boy" in the *Mr. Peabody's Improbable History* segments of *Rocky and His Friends*. Bill Scott, voice of Bullwinkle, Fearless Leader, Dudley Do-Right and others, projected his precise, Clifton Webb-type speech as lead dog Peabody, a pedantic white beagle who always wore a small red bow tie and thick spectacles.

Walter, of course, did his Leroy voice for the freckled, bespectacled, innocent little cartoon boy, Sherman.

Created by Ted Key (famous as the artist-creator of Hazel), the pun-filled cartoons began in 1959. The crudely-drawn Jay Ward animation had brilliant scripts (mostly written by Chris Hayward) of dog and boy meeting everyone from Napoleon to Confucius to Tom Thumb. They would time travel via the WABAC Machine to correct any history that was veering off the path toward catastrophe; the adventures would usually end in a pun bad enough to crack Sherman's thick glasses.

Before the famous and well-defined characters became Peabody and Sherman, the segment had been called *Danny Daydream*. Creator Ted Key explained: "Day dreaming is just another way to travel. You can go anywhere in the world, meet anyone who ever lived, invent, explore, party, fight, love, conquer, achieve, without spending a dime. It's a short cut to adventure, and thrills. A quick way to get out of the house. And if you're doing it on TV, as a kid named Danny did, you can take your whole audience with you. Kids like yourself, or adults who are, in heart, still kids.

"But just being Danny Daydream wasn't enough. The 'concept' needed a 'kicker.' A fresh slant – so I gave him a take-charge companion.

Daydream was an underlying concept, not a name, and too obvious. Time travel, not daydreaming, was introduced. Lists of names submitted. Names chosen. The 'people,' and 'events,' to 'get to.' I was delighted with the 'characters' they finally went with. I established the 'characters,' but Jay Ward and his brilliant, inventive staff chose their 'missions.' They brought them to life, and I was pleased with the way they did it. More than pleased. Happy, and supportive. I thought Walter Tetley's voice was perfect for Sherman. Bill Scott and Jay Ward made the right choices. They didn't submit tests of Walter to me; nor of any of the voices. But the choices they did make were perfect.

"Years have passed since the show first took a bow. I was as delighted with it then as I still am now.

"It's my feeling that if there had been no 'Peabody and Sherman' segment, the Rocky and Bullwinkle Show would not have been on TV at all. It might not have been bought.

"My reasoning:

"Jay Ward came East, to New York City, with a five minute pilot of the Rocky and Bullwinkle show. The ad agency and sponsor liked it. 'What're you going to do with the other 25 minutes?' they asked Jay. He didn't know. He didn't have the money for a longer pilot or another 'segment' to add to his *five minute* show.

"He became ill. He asked me if I could come up with something. I said, 'I'll *try*, Jay.' He flew back to the West Coast. Had a nervous breakdown, after turning over the project to my brother. (We were all neighbors and friends in Berkeley, California.) Somehow money was raised for the Peabody and Sherman pilot. The advertising agency *loved* it, and based on that discussion, decided to go ahead with the *whole half hour project*. Jay found Bill Scott to build up his West Cost studio and the show was on its way."

Courtesy of Ward Productions, Inc.

The first show, in which they met Ben Franklin, told the origin of boy and dog getting together: Peabody cast off his professorial guise for a moment to bark at the bullies beating up poor Sherman in an alley. Grateful, the little kid followed the dog home. Tetley voiced all ninety-one 4.5 minute episodes of *Mr. Peabody's Improbable History*, which still remains one of the most beloved components of *Rocky and His Friends*.

When the Golden LP, *Rocky and His Friends*, was released in 1960, Tetley/Sherman was given a solo number to sing. "I Wanna Go Back with the WABAC Machine" was a fun little novelty number harkening Tetley back to his vaudeville days. He also appeared in two Peabody adventures (meeting Ponce de Leon, and when Stanley met Livingston), and joined others in the rousing introductory song, "Peabody's History."

On February 15, 1970 Hal Peary wrote to a fan:

“Walter Tetley, who played ‘LEROY’ for many years on the radio series, even with Waterman, is hospitalized at the Los Angeles County U.S.C. Medical Center, Ward 3700, 1200 N. State St., Los Angeles, Calif. 90033. Tetley was injured while riding a motorcycle—has two broken legs, two broken arms and a fractured pelvis. He will be there for at least two more months.”

Early in 1970 while riding his motorcycle near Van Nuys Walter was struck head-on by a motorist who failed to stop for a traffic light. He suffered internal injuries that put him in pain for the rest of his life.

On February 26, 1970 Peary wrote again to the fan: “Thanks for writing to Walter Tetley and for your trouble in asking others to do so. I know that he will enjoy all the communications. He is pretty lonely in that plaster of paris underwear and the pulleys…”

In April Walter was moved to Olive View Hospital, Ward 301, at 14701 Foothill Boulevard in Los Angeles County. He was there for at least 3 months.

Ailing though he was, Walter still wanted to work, and was grateful for the few opportunities that came his way. Don Pitts, his last agent, remembered the sad situation.

“When I got in the business, I looked him up, I was always his fan, but he didn't want to do anything at all. He was working in a pet shop in the Valley someplace. I talked him into coming in. He had no money. He ended up in Olive View Hospital and his insurance at SAG had run out, so he was destitute.

"I submitted him to Hanna-Barbera one day, for a kid's part, submitted him to Alex Loathy who had been out there forever, so I certainly assumed he knew who the hell Walter Tetley was. I brought in a tape I had Walter make, just before his accident. I played the tape, and Alex said, 'Yeah, he sounds kinda like what I'm looking for.' So I set up the interview, but Walter was still in the hospital, so they were going to take him in an ambulance to the interview. He told the hospital if he could get this job, that whatever wages he earned could be applied against his bill. After the audition, Alex called from Hanna-Barbera and he was furious with me. 'How could you do this to me?' he shouted. I said, 'What are you talking about? Didn't he show up?' He said, 'I've never been so embarrassed in my whole life. I thought this was a kid! I was told he was in the lobby so I ran out there and here was this old man in a wheel chair with his leg up in a cast and a couple of attendants in white outfits standing with him. I said to the receptionist, "Where is Mrs. Tetley and her son?"' I asked, 'Well, how did he sound?' Alex said he sounded fine, just like the tape, but no, he wanted a kid!

"Alex said he wanted some tapes of other kids, and I gave him one of my son, who ended up getting the job. And I felt so badly I told Walter the story, and he said, 'My whole life has been like that, Don. Once they *saw* me, I never got the job.'

One of many publicity stills for Tetley's clown act.

"Walter said, 'They used to have a little suit for me over at Western Costume. It was a bellboy's suit, and whenever they had a bellboy's role in a feature film, they would just call over and get the suit, and I would get the call. But when the business changed, and they saw me, they just wouldn't hire me.' It was a very sad story. He was a super nice guy. A wonderful talent.

"When I was looking for him originally, everyone referred to him as 'little Walter.' When he came into the office to work with me, he was full grown, but unfortunately he had a very yellow, jaundice-like complexion. Very, very leathery looking skin, with these deep wrinkles. I'm sure it was all part of his condition."

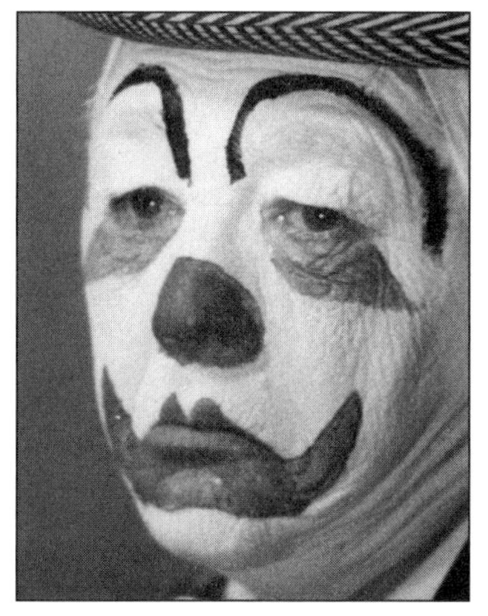

Satirist/comedian Stan Freberg made much the same comment after working with Tetley for recording sessions for a comedy album. The voice actor's discolored and badly wrinkled skin was probably the result of the hormone injections he had received years earlier in treatment for his retarded growth.

Walter's unfortunate appearance in his later years may have accounted for his decision to do a clown act for children. By doing so he could hide behind layers of thick make-up. The act was not performed for professional reasons, he used it solely to entertain shut-in friends as well as patients in the children's ward of various hospitals. He sometimes appeared with a female clown partner. Other than wearing the clown make-up, it is not known exactly of what the act consisted.

The clown act idea had occurred to him sometime in the late 1950's before his debilitating motorcycle accident. Among the few mementos saved from his later years that were found in his scrapbooks are a number photographs in clown make-up.

After Walter had been hospitalized for nearly a year, he came out of the accident having to walk with a cane, and later was confined to a wheelchair.

Luckily his physical condition and skin complaints were overcome enough to have secured a few jobs in his last years.

On December 9, 1972 Walter's new Hanna-Barbera cartoon special, *A Christmas Story*, aired. Tetley played Timmy who had written a letter to Santa which had accidentally fallen behind a table. When a kind-hearted mouse called Gumdrop (voiced by Daws Butler) found it, he and Timmy's huge dog Goober (voiced by Paul Winchell) sought out Santa Claus to give him the

letter. They escaped the terror of four mischievous cats and finally found Santa descending a chimney. To reach him Gumdrop put the letter in a glider and sailed it towards his sleigh. It sailed too high and went over the roof into the snow. Dejected, the two friends returned home and fell asleep. Later, they were awakened by the joyous shouts of Timmy who was thrilled to find his special request granted: "Peace on Earth" was written in the sky by the magical glow of Santa's sleigh. As Santa left, he yelled, "Merry Christmas to all, and to all a good night." It was just the sort of wish Walter Tetley himself would have asked for.

The cast of voices was one of the best assembled. Janet Waldo played the mother/girl. Don Messick, the dad and squirrel. Hal Smith was Santa and Fatcat, with John Stephenson as Polecat, Postman and First Dog. The special was written by Ken Spears and Joe Ruby, dotted with songs ("Christmas Story," "Hope," "Where Do You Love?" and "Which One is the Real Santa Claus?") by Denby Williams and Joseph Roland.

The recording was fun, but painful for Walter who continued to complain about the pain in his legs. But he needed to get back on track financially after all the doctor and hospital bills. Most of all, he needed to keep mentally active. Voicing commercials was lucrative, if difficult to obtain. Around 1973 he was heard as a newspaper boy in a Keebler's cookie commercial.

Tetley's last radio work was on a five-part episode of *The Hollywood Radio Theater* entitled "The Princess Stakes Murder." This unique series was narrated by Rod Sterling and was one of the last recorded syndicated series aired over the Mutual Network.

But apart from the odd job, no one knew what had happened to Walter or where he was living. Paul Frees thought he was living in a trailer near the beach.

On June 17, 1975 Walter was admitted to the Beverly Manor Convalescent Hospital at 7940 Topanga Canyon Boulevard in Canoga Park,

California. On September 7, 1975 at 12:25 a.m. Walter Campbell Tetley died there. He was 60 years old. The death certificate stated, "Approximate interval between onset and death – 10 weeks." He gave his last employer as Hanna-Barbera and his last/usual address as 22858 Collins Street in Woodland Hills, Los Angeles. Though he may have been living at the Encino Oaks Motor Lodge free of charge, as it was run by Tetley's friend Jack W. Butts. There was no autopsy, and no family survivors. Walter was cremated on September 10, 1975 at Oakwood Memorial Park, and the remains were buried there.

Services were held at 2 p.m. at Reseda Masonic Temple on 6701 Darby Avenue where Walter was an active member. Interment was private.

Jack W. Butts, owner/manager of the Encino Oaks Motor Lodge at 17323 Ventura Blvd. was named executor of Tetley's estate. One of Walter's last wishes was that any monies owed to him by the Screen Actors Guild (he was member #13696 of the Los Angeles branch) for his film work was to go to the Boy Scott troop he helped establish. $2800 was secured from his pension fund and given to the troop.

Epilogue, or How This Book Came To Be

Charles Stumpf, who for years compiled information for the definitive book on Fibber McGee and Molly entitled *Heavenly Days*, had been in touch with various cast members associated with the program. Among those interviewed was Hal Peary.

"In November of the year that Walter Tetley died," Stumpf explained, "I was contacted by Jack Butts, the executor of his estate, at the suggestion of Hal Peary, asking if I could help compile a list of Tetley's film credits between the years 1938 and 1959, in order that a death benefit could be obtained from the Screen Actor's Guild, which would then be donated to one of Walter's favorite charities. I was indeed happy to comply. On April 4, 1976 I was informed that a death benefit had been obtained and donated to the Rainbow Scholarship Fund of the Boy Scouts, to aid handicapped children.

"At the time I asked Jack Butts if there might be any photographs or anything else pertaining to Walter's career that were to be disposed of. In response, Mr. Butts sent me two old scrapbooks of photos and clippings covering his career, that had been kept by his parents. I was also sent a small black notebook in which Walter's father had kept a careful accounting of each of his appearances—beginning with the very first radio show on February 9, 1930. The book also includes dates of auditions that Walter did, and is complete through April 13, 1938. In that span of time the ambitious young actor had chalked up 2,961 appearances—and that was just the beginning of his long career.

"These priceless items are excellent reference material as well as treasured momentos of a most distinguished career. I shall be eternally grateful to Mr. Butts for his kindness."

Ben Ohmart commented:

"Writing a book on Tetley 25 years after the scrapbooks were turned over to Stumpf proved difficult in assembling supplementary material. Mr. Butts' only known address was for the Encino Oaks Motor Lodge which he had operated in Encino, California. We tried to contact him there, but to no avail. We contacted the Encino Chamber of Commerce but they were unable to furnish any further leads. Nor were they able to supply any information whatsoever about Tetley's pet shop, The Happy Tail. The Boy Scouts were unable to provide any information on the Rainbow Troop that Walter had founded and worked for."

The quest for information beyond that contained in the scrapbooks and notebook led to more dead ends. There are no known surviving family members. Contacts with any of Walter's former co-workers divulged very little. They all had very favorable things to say about him and his work—but no one really seemed to have known him well. Walter was a very private person and shunned the limelight.

Upon contact, the Screen Actor's Guild replied, "If Mr. Tetley did not do any work on a SAG signatory film that commenced AFTER January 31, 1960, there will be no residuals to his estate." Since Walter's only recurring work after 1960 appears to have been with the Jay Ward animated cartoon series for television, and SAG did not have to keep his estate information on file, obviously nothing was, or is, being paid into the estate.

Anyone reading this book with any information that can possibly fill in any of the gaps in Walter's life story, again, please get in touch.

Parts of Walter Tetley's life may remain a mystery. But one thing is certain. "Leroy," "Julius," "Sherman" and all of his many other characters will forever live on to delight new generations to come. Comic genius will be recognized.

The Authors
September 2003

Acknowledgements

Thanks be to the following people for their help in uncovering some of the mysteries of WT: Dick Beals, Bill Bell, Conrad Binyon, Terry L. Black, Earl Diamond, June Foray, Eric Frazier, Jack French, Larry Gassman, David Goldin, Martin Grams, Jr., Tim Hollis, Ted & Bonnie Key, Brian Kistler, Bill Kizer, Regina Kramer, Shirley Mitchell, Hal Peary, Don Pitts, Jay Rath, Terry Salomonson, Keith Scott, Jon G. Smith, Charles Ulrich, Laura Wagner, Willard Waterman, Mike Wheeler, and Roberta Zonghi.

CREDITS

LISTED IN THE LITTLE BLACK NOTEBOOK

RADIO SHOWS

1930:

February 9	Children's Hour
February 15	Barn Show [With Madge Tucker]
February 16	Children's Hour
February 22	Barn Show
February 23	Children's Hour
July 13	Children's Hour
July 17	Lady Next Door
July 19	Lady Next Door
July 20	Children's Hour
July 23	Lady Next Door
July 26	Lady Next Door
July 27	Children's Hour
August 1	Lady Next Door
August 2	Lady Next Door
August 3	Children's Hour
August 7	Lady Next Door
August 9	Lady Next Door

[Titles in ( ) have no show number listed, therefore they are public appearances or auditions. Though the notebook lists what show number this was for Walter, as they are all consecutive we have left these numbers out. When a number appears in ( ) after a show title, it usually denotes a repeat broadcast for the west coast. Walter's first radio show was the February 9, 1930 *Children's Hour*. The first page is missing in this notebook, but all shows are consecutive starting on July 13, which was Walter's 49th show.

The credits have been kept as they were originally written in the notebook, with author notes in [ ] for the sake of clarity. P.A. = personal appearance.]

August 10	Children's Hour
August 11	Lady Next Door
August 17	Children's Hour
August 20	Lady Next Door
August 23	Lady Next Door
August 24	Children's Hour
August 27	Lady Next Door
August 28	Lady Next Door
August 31	Children's Hour
September 1	Lady Next Door
September 3	Lady Next Door
September 6	Lady Next Door
September 7	Children's Hour
September 12	Lady Next Door
September 13	Lady Next Door
September 14	Children's Hour
September 15	Lady Next Door
September 17	Lady Next Door
September 20	Lady Next Door
September 21	Children's Hour
September 24	Lady Next Door
September 25	Lady Next Door
September 27	Lady Next Door
September 28	Children's Hour
September 30	Lady Next Door
October 1	Lady Next Door
October 4	Lady Next Door
October 4	Dixie Circus
October 5	Children's Hour
October 8	Lady Next Door
October 10	Lady Next Door
October 12	Children's Hour
October 13	Lady Next Door
October 18	Lady Next Door
October 19	Children's Hour
October 22	Lady Next Door
October 23	Lady Next Door
October 24	Lady Next Door

October 25	Lady Next Door
October 26	Children's Hour
October 29	Lady Next Door
October 30	Lady Next Door
October 31	Lady Next Door
November 1	Lady Next Door
November 2	Children's Hour
November 3	Lady Next Door
November 5	Lady Next Door
November 6	Lady Next Door
November 8	Household
November 8	Lady Next Door
November 9	Children's Hour
November 13	Lady Next Door
November 15	Lady Next Door
November 16	Children's Hour
November 19	Lady Next Door
November 20	Lady Next Door
November 21	Lady Next Door
November 22	Lady Next Door
November 23	Children's Hour
November 26	Lady Next Door
November 28	Lady Next Door
November 28	Mason J.C. [P.A. – People's Palace, Jersey City, NJ]
November 30	Children's Hour
December 1	Lady Next Door
December 3	Lady Next Door
December 5	Lady Next Door
December 5	Yonkers [P.A.]
December 7	Children's Hour
December 8	Lady Next Door
December 9	Lady Next Door
December 10	Lady Next Door
December 13	Lady Next Door
December 14	Children's Hour
December 15	Lady Next Door
December 17	Lady Next Door

December 18	Lady Next Door
December 20	Lady Next Door
December 21	Children's Hour
December 22	Lady Next Door
December 23	Lady Next Door
December 24	Lady Next Door
December 25	Lady Next Door
December 27	Lady Next Door
December 28	Children's Hour
December 29	Lady Next Door
December 30	Lady Next Door
1931:	
January 3	Lady Next Door
January 4	Children's Hour
January 5	Lady Next door
January 7	Lady Next Door
January 8	Lady Next Door
January 10	Lady Next Door
January 10	Eastern Star [National Women's Organization. Installation dinner at Pythian Temple, New York City]
January 11	Children's Hour
January 12	Lady Next Door
January 15	Lady Next Door
January 17	Lady Next Door
January 18	Children's Hour
January 19	Lady Next Door
January 23	Lady Next Door
January 24	Lady Next Door
January 25	Children's Hour
January 26	Lady Next Door
January 29	Lady Next Door
January 31	Lady Next Door
February 1	Children's Hour
February 2	Lady Next Door
February 4	Lady Next Door
February 5	Lady Next Door

February 5	Raising Jr.
February 6	Raising Jr.
February 7	Lady Next Door
February 7	Dixie Circus
February 7	Ku Ku Hour [The Cukoo Hour]
February 8	Children's Hour
February 9	Lady Next Door
February 11	Raising Jr.
February 12	Lady Next Door
February 14	Lady Next Door
February 15	Children's Hour
February 16	Lady Next Door
February 19	Lady Next Door
February 19	Raising Jr.
February 21	Scranton, PA [P.A. Jr. O.U.A. Country Club]
February 22	Children's Hour
February 23	Maltine
February 24	Lady Next Door
February 26	Lady Next door
February 26	Niaraga Hudson
February 27	Raising Jr.
February 27	Uncle Abe & David
February 28	Lady Next Door
March 1	Children's Hour
March 2	Lady Next Door
March 4	Lady Next Door
March 4	Raising Jr.
March 5	Lady Next Door
March 5	Rapid Transit [These are possibly live radio commercials]
March 6	Lady Next Door
March 7	Lady Next Door
March 8	Children's Hour
March 8	Raising Jr.
March 9	Lady Next Door
March 10	Rapid Transit
March 11	Lady Next Door

March 11	(Yonkers)
March 12	Lady Next Door
March 13	Lady Next Door
March 14	Lady Next Door
March 14	(Eastern Star M.C.)
March 15	Children's Hour
March 16	Lady Next Door
March 18	Lady Next Door
March 19	Lady Next Door
March 21	Lady Next Door
March 22	Children's Hour
March 23	Lady Next Door
March 25	Lady Next Door
March 26	Lady Next Door
March 26	Rapid Transit
March 28	Lady Next Door
March 29	Children's Hour
March 30	Lady Next Door
March 30	Raising Jr.
March 31	Rapid Transit
April 1	Lady Next Door
April 2	Lady Next Door
April 2	Rapid Transit
April 4	Lady Next Door
April 5	Children's Hour
April 6	Lady Next Door
April 7	(Rockville Center) [Benefit for South Nassau Community Hospital in New York]
April 8	Lady Next Door
April 9	Lady Next Door
April 9	Rapid Transit
April 11	Lady Next Door
April 11	(Eastern Star M.C.)
April 12	Children's Hour
April 13	Lady Next Door
April 15	Lady Next Door
April 16	Lady Next Door

April 18	Lady Next Door
April 18	Ku Ku Hour
April 19	Children's Hour
April 19	Colliers Hour
April 20	Lady Next Door
April 22	Lady Next Door
April 23	Lady Next Door
April 25	Lady Next Door
April 26	Children's Hour
April 27	Lady Next Door
April 28	Raising Jr.
April 29	Lady Next Door
April 30	Lady Next Door
May 1	(Pottstown, PA) [At the Victor Theater]
May 2	Lady Next Door
May 2	(Union City Mason)
May 3	Children's Hour
May 4	Lady Next Door
May 6	(Morris Plan, NJ)
May 7	Lady Next Door
May 8	(Audition)
May 9	Lady Next Door
May 10	Children's Hour
May 10	Mother's Days [Probably special "Mother's Day" broadcast]
May 10	National Dairy
May 11	Lady Next Door
May 11	(Audition)
May 13	Lady Next Door
May 13	Raising Jr.
May 14	Lady Next Door
May 16	Lady Next Door
May 17	Children's Hour
May 18	Lady Next Door
May 20	Lady Next Door
May 21	Lady Next Door
May 22	Lady Next Door
May 22	Raising Jr.

May 23	Lady Next Door
May 23	(St. Mitz. Nurses)
May 24	Children's Hour
May 25	Eno [The Eno Crime Club]
May 25	Lady Next Door
May 26	Eno
May 27	Lady Next Door
May 27	Eno
May 28	Lady Next Door
May 28	Eno
May 29	Eno
May 30	Lady Next Door
May 30	Eno
May 31	Children's Hour
June 1	Lux [Lux Radio Theater]
June 3	Lady Next Door
June 4	Lady Next Door
June 5	Lady Next Door
June 6	Lady Next Door
June 7	Children's Hour
June 8	Lady Next Door
June 9	Raising Jr.
June 10	Lady Next Door
June 12	Raising Jr.
June 13	Lady Next Door
June 14	Children's Hour
June 14	Emerald Isle
June 15	Lady Next Door
June 17	(Audition)
June 18	Lady Next Door
June 20	Lady Next Door
June 21	Children's Hour
June 22	Lady Next Door
June 23	Raising Jr.
June 23	(Audition)
June 24	Lady Next Door
June 25	Lady Next Door
June 26	Lady Next Door

June 27-30	(Franklin Theatre)
July 2	Lady Next Door
July 3	Lady Next Door
July 3	Raising Jr.
July 4	(Bayville)
July 5	Children's Hour
July 5	Emerald Isle
July 5	(Trenton, NJ)
July 8	Lady Next Door
July 9	Lady Next Door
July 9	Niaraga Hudson [P.A.]
July 11	Lady Next Door
July 12	Children's Hour
July 12	Emerald Isle
July 12	(Mrs. Seeley Flusing) [P.A. Flushing, NY]
July 13	Lady Next Door
July 15	Lady Next Door
July 16	Allentown, PA [P.A. Picnic for St. Paul's Lutheran Sunday school]
July 17	Raising Jr.
July 18	Lady Next Door
July 19	Children's Hour
July 20	Lady Next Door
July 22-24	(86 St. Theatre)
July 25	(Adamstown, PA)
July 26	Children's Hour
July 27	Lady Next Door
July 28	Raising Jr.
July 29	Lady Next Door
July 30	Lady Next Door
August 1	Lady Next Door
August 2	Children's Hour
August 2	Emerald Isle
August 2	(Trenton, NJ)
August 3	(Audition)
August 5	Lady Next Door
August 6	Lady Next Door
August 8	Lady Next Door

August 9	Children's Hour
August 9	Emerald Isle
August 10	Lady Next Door
August 11	Raising Jr.
August 12-13	(Claramont, NY)
August 15	(Adamstown, PA)
August 16	Children's Hour
August 17	Lady Next Door
August 18	Lady Next Door
August 20	Lady Next Door
August 21	Lady Next Door
August 22	Lady Next Door
August 23	Children's Hour
August 24	Lady Next Door
August 26	Lady Next Door
August 26	(Audition)
August 27	Lady Next Door
August 27	(Audition)
August 28	Lady Next Door
August 29	Constitution Trip
August 30	Emerald Isle
August 31	Lady Next Door
September 1	Lady Next Door
September 1	(Flushing Rotary)
September 2	Lady Next Door
September 3	Lady Next Door
September 3	(Audition)
September 6	Children's Hour
September 6	Emerald Isle
September 7	True Story
September 8	Lady Next Door
September 9	Lady Next Door
September 9	Women's Radio Rev.
September 10	Lady Next Door
September 11	Lady Next Door
September 12	Lady Next Door
September 13	Children's Hour
September 13	Emerald Isle

September 14	Lady Next Door
September 15	Lady Next Door
September 15	(Audition)
September 15	Raising Jr.
September 16	Household [Big Time Radio Household]
September 16	(Asbury Park)
September 17	(Audition)
September 19	Lady Next Door
September 20	Children's Hour
September 23	Lady Next Door
September 24	Lady Next Door
September 25	(Washington D.C.)
September 26	Lady Next Door
September 27	Children's Hour
September 27	Emerald Isle
September 28	Lady Next Door
September 30	Lady Next Door
October 1	Lady Next Door
October 4	Children's Hour
October 5	True Story
October 6	Maltine
October 7	Bordens
October 7	Lady Next Door
October 8	Lady Next Door
October 8	Raising Jr.
October 11	Children's Hour
October 11	Emerald Isle
October 12	Lady Next Door
October 13	Maltine
October 14	Lady Next Door
October 15	Lady Next Door
October 17	Lady Next Door
October 18	Children's Hour
October 18	Emerald Isle
October 19	Lady Next Door
October 20	Lady Next Door
October 21	Lady Next Door
October 22	Lady Next Door

October 25	Children's Hour
October 25	Emerald Isle
October 26	Lady Next Door
October 28	Lady Next Door
October 29	Lady Next Door
October 30	Lady Next Door
October 30	General Electric
October 31	Lady Next Door
November 1	Children's Hour
November 1	Emerald Isle
November 3	Lady Next Door
November 3	Raising Jr.
November 5	Lady Next Door
November 6	Lady Next Door
November 6	General Electric
November 7	Lady Next Door
November 8	Children's Hour
November 8	Emerald Isle
November 9	Lady Next Door
November 10	Raising Jr.
November 11	Household
November 12	Lady Next Door
November 13	Lady Next Door
November 14	(Eastern Star)
November 15	Children's Hour
November 15	Emerald Isle
November 16	Lady Next Door
November 16	True Story
November 18	Lady Next Door
November 19	Lady Next Door
November 20	Lady Next Door
November 20	March of Time
November 21	Lady Next Door
November 22	Children's Hour
November 22	Emerald Isle
November 22	Raising Jr.
November 23	Lady Next Door
November 23	True Story

November 25	Lady Next Door
November 27	Lady Next Door
November 27	Raising Jr.
November 28	Lady Next Door
November 29	Children's Hour
November 29	Emerald Isle
November 30	Lady Next Door
November 30	Raising Jr.
December 2	Lady Next Door
December 3	Lady Next Door
December 4	Raising Jr.
December 5	Lady Next Door
December 6	Children's Hour
December 6	Emerald Isle
December 7	Lady Next Door
December 7	Raising Jr.
December 8	Maltine
December 9	(Hightstown, N.J.)
December 13	Raising Jr.
December 14	Lady Next Door
December 16	Lady Next Door
December 18	Lady Next Door
December 19	Lady Next Door
December 19	Raising Jr.
December 20	Children's Hour
December 20	Emerald Isle
December 21	Lady Next Door
December 22	Maltine
December 23	Lady Next Door
December 24	Lady Next Door
December 25	Lady Next Door
December 25	Lady Next Door C.P. (Command Performance?)
December 27	Children's Hour
December 27	Emerald Isle
December 27	Raising Jr.
December 28	Lady Next Door
December 28	Raising Jr.

December 29	Lady Next Door
December 30	Lady Next Door
December 31	Children's Hour

1932:

January 1	Raising Jr.
January 2	Lady Next Door
January 3	Children's Hour
January 3	Emerald Isle
January 3	Raising Jr.
January 4	Lady Next Door
January 5	Maltine
January 6	Lady Next Door
January 9	Raising Jr.
January 10	Children's Hour
January 10	Emerald Isle
January 11	Lady Next Door
January 12	Maltine
January 13	Lady Next Door
January 14	Lady Next Door
January 14	Raising Jr.
January 16	Lady Next Door
January 17	Children's Hour
January 17	Emerald Isle
January 18	Lady Next Door
January 20	Lady Next Door
January 22	Lady Next Door
January 22	Raising Jr.
January 24	Children's Hour
January 24	Emerald Isle
January 25	Lady Next Door
January 26	Lady Next Door
January 27	Lady Next Door
January 28	Lady Next Door
January 29	Raising Jr.
January 30	Household
January 30	Lady Next Door
January 31	Children's Hour

January 31	Emerald Isle
February 1	Lady Next Door
February 1	Raising Jr.
February 3	Lady Next Door
February 4	Lady Next Door
February 7	Lady Next Door
February 7	Children's Hour
February 9	Raising Jr.
February 10	Lady Next Door
February 12	Lady Next Door
February 13	Raising Jr.
February 14	Children's Hour
February 15	Lady Next Door
February 17	Lady Next Door
February 18	Lady Next Door
February 19	Raising Jr.
February 20	Lady Next Door
February 21	Children's Hour
February 21	Emerald Isle
February 21	Raising Jr.
February 22	Raising Jr.
February 23	Lady Next Door
February 25	Lady Next Door
February 26	Lady Next Door
February 28	Children's Hour
February 28	Emerald Isle
February 29	Lady Next Door
March 2	Lady Next Door
March 4	Friendship Town
March 5	Lady Next Door
March 5	Raising Jr.
March 6	Children's Hour
March 7	Lady Next Door
March 9	Lady Next Door
March 10	Lady Next Door
March 10	Raising Jr.
March 11	Lady Next Door
March 12	Lady Next Door

March 13	Children's Hour
March 14	Lady Next Door
March 16	Lady Next Door
March 17	Lady Next Door
March 20	Children's Hour
March 21	Lady Next Door
March 21	Raising Jr.
March 23	Lady Next Door
March 24	Lady Next Door
March 26	Lady Next Door
March 27	Children's Hour
March 28	Lady Next Door
March 30	Lady Next Door
April 1	Friendship Town
April 2	Lady Next Door
April 3	Children's Hour
April 4	Lady Next Door
April 5	Household
April 5	(Hackensack, NJ)
April 6	Lady Next Door
April 9	Lady Next Door
April 9	Raising Jr.
April 10	Children's Hour
April 11	Children's Hour
April 13	Lady Next Door
April 14	Lady Next Door
April 15	(Coaldale, PA)
April 17	Children's Hour
April 17	Raising Jr.
April 18	Lady Next Door
April 18	Household
April 19	Lady Next Door
April 21	Lady Next Door
April 22	(Kingstown, PA) [P.A. Band concert in high school auditorium]
April 23	Lady Next Door
April 24	Children's Hour
April 25	Lady Next Door

April 26	(Bogato, NJ)
April 27	Lady Next Door
April 25 (or 28)	Household
April 28	Du Pont
April 29	Household
April 30	Lady Next Door
April 30	Hap Tulliver
May 1	Children's Hour
May 2	Lady Next Door
May 4	Lady Next Door
May 6	Friendship Town
May 7	Lady Next Door
May 7	Hap Tulliver
May 8	Children's Hour
May 9	Lady Next Door
May 11	Lady Next Door
May 12	Lady Next Door
May 14	(Lowlow, MA) [Ludlow, MA]
May 15	Children's Hour
May 16	Household
May 18	Lady Next Door
May 19	Lady Next Door
May 21	Lady Next Door
May 22	Children's Hour
May 23	Household
May 23	Lady Next Door
May 25	Lady Next Door
May 26	Lady Next Door
May 28	Lady Next Door
May 29	Children's Hour
May 30	Lady Next Door
June 1	Lady Next Door
June 2	Lady Next Door
June 4	Lady Next Door
June 5	Children's Hour
June 6	Household
June 6	Lady Next Door
June 6	Tasty Yeast

June 7	Lady Next Door
June 8	Mother's Day
June 8	Lady Next Door
June 10	Friendship Town
June 12	Children's Hour
June 13	Household
June 13	Lady Next Door
June 13	Tasty Yeast
June 15	Big Time
June 15	Lady Next Door
June 17	Friendship Town
June 18	Lady Next Door
June 19	Children's Hour
June 19	Father's Day
June 20	Lady Next Door
June 20	(audition)
June 22	Lady Next Door
June 23	Lady Next Door
June 24	Lady Next Door
June 25	Lady Next Door
June 26	Children's Hour
June 27	Lady Next Door
June 27	Tasty Yeast
June 28	?
June 28	Joe Palooka
June 29	Lady Next Door
June 30	Lady Next Door
July 1	Lady Next Door
July 2	(audition)
July 3	Children's Hour
July 4	Household
July 5	Lady Next Door
July 6	Lady Next Door
July 8	Lady Next Door
July 8	(audition)
July 9	Lady Next Door
July 9	East Lynn
July 10	Children's Hour

July 11	Household
July 11	Lady Next Door
July 12	Lady Next Door
July 13	Lady Next Door
July 14	Lady Next Door
July 15	Lady Next Door
July 16	Lady Next Door
July 17	Children's Hour
July 18	Household
July 18	Lady Next Door
July 19	Lady Next Door
July 20	Lady Next Door
July 21	Lady Next Door
July 22	(Claremont, NY)
July 24	Children's Hour
July 25	Household
July 26	Skyscraper
July 27	Lady Next Door
July 28	Lady Next Door
July 29	Lady Next Door
July 30	Lady Next Door
July 31	Children's Hour
August 1	Lady Next Door
August 2	Lady Next Door
August 3	Lady Next Door
August 4	(New Rochelle) [P.A. in New York]
August 5	Lady Next Door
August 6	Lady Next Door
August 7	Children's Hour
August 7	Silver Flute
August 8	Lady Next Door
August 8	Household
August 9	Lady Next Door
August 10	(audition)
August 12	Lady Next Door
August 13	Lady Next Door
August 14	Children's Hour
August 15	Household

August 15	Lady Next Door
August 16	Lady Next Door
August 18	Lady Next Door
August 22	Household
August 22	Lady Next Door
August 23	Lady Next Door
August 25	Lady Next Door
August 26	Lady Next Door
August 27	Lady Next Door
August 28	Children's Hour
August 28	Chase & Sanborn
August 29	Household
August 29	Lady Next Door
August 31	Lady Next Door
September 4	Children's Hour
September 4	Household
September 5	Lady Next Door
September 6	Lady Next Door
September 8	Lady Next Door
September 9	Lady Next Door
September 11	Children's Hour
September 12	Household
September 13	Lady Next Door
September 14	Lady Next Door
September 15	Lady Next Door
September 16	Lady Next Door
September 16	(mike test)
September 18	Children's Hour
September 20	Friendship Town
September 21	Lady Next Door
September 22	Lady Next Door
September 23	Lady Next Door
September 24	Lady Next Door
September 25	Children's Hour
September 26	Revolving Stage
September 26	Lady Next Door
September 27	Lady Next Door
September 28	Lady Next Door

September 29	Lady Next Door
September 30	Lady Next Door
October 2	Children's Hour
October 3	Lady Next Door
October 5	Lady Next Door
October 6	Household
October 6	Lady Next Door
October 8	Littmann's [Possibly commercial for the large department store]
October 9	Children's Hour
October 10	Lady Next Door
October 11	Wheatenaville
October 12	Flying Family
October 13	Household
October 13	Lady Next Door
October 14	Littmann's
October 14	Wayside Cottage
October 14	Lady Next Door
October 15	Lady Next Door
October 16	Children's Hour
October 17	Lady Next Door
October 17	(audition)
October 17	(audition)
October 18	Lady Next Door
October 19	Lady Next Door
October 20	Lady Next Door
October 20	Household
October 21	Records [Recording transcribed shows]
October 22	Littmann's
October 22	(audition)
October 22	Records
October 23	Children's Hour
October 24	Lady Next Door
October 24	(audition)
October 25	Lady Next Door
October 26	Lady Next Door
October 27	Records
October 27	Household

October 29	Lady Next Door
October 30	Children's Hour
October 31	Wayside Cottage
October 31	(audition)
November 1	Records
November 2	Flying Family
November 2	Lady Next Door
November 3	Household
November 3	Country Doctor
November 4	Lady Next Door
November 4	Unemployed [Possibly a commercial for the Unemployment Office]
November 5	Littmann's
November 5	Lady Next Door
November 6	Children's Hour
November 7	Lady Next Door
November 8	Lady Next Door
November 9	Lady Next Door
November 10	Household
November 10	Death Valley Days
November 11	Lady Next Door
November 11	March of Time
November 12	Prospect Theatre
November 13	Prospect Theatre
November 14	Prospect Theatre
November 15	Prospect Theatre
November 16	Lady Next Door
November 16	Wheatenaville
November 17	Lady Next Door
November 17	(Eastern Star E.W.)
November 18	(audition)
November 18	Lady Next Door
November 18	(Yonkers P.T.A.)
November 19	Littmann's
November 20	Children's Hour
November 21	Records (two)
November 22	Lady Next Door
November 23	Records (three)

November 24	Death Valley Days
November 25	Lady Next Door
November 25	March of Time
November 26	Littmann's
November 26	Lady Next Door
November 27	Children's Hour
November 27	Red Adams
November 28	Wheatenaville
November 29	(audition)
November 29	(bazaar)
November 30	(Pathe)
November 30	Records
December 1	Lady Next Door
December 2	Lady Next Door
December 2	March of Time
December 2	(audition)
December 2	(pipe band)
December 3	Littmann's
December 3	Lady Next Door
December 4	Children's Hour
December 4	Red Adams
December 5	(audition)
December 7	Lady Next Door
December 7	(audition)
December 7	(audition)
December 7	(audition)
December 8	Lady Next Door
December 8	(audition)
December 8	(audition)
December 9	Lady Next Door
December 9	(Newark Church)
December 10	Littmann's
December 10	Lady Next Door
December 11	Children's Hour
December 12	Hitting the Keys [Probably a local radio show]
December 12	Records
December 13	(audition)

December 14	Hitting the Keys
December 15	(audition)
December 16	Hitting the Keys
December 16	Records (2)
December 16	Unemployed
December 17	Littmann's
December 18	Children's Hour
December 21	Lady Next Door
December 22	Lady Next Door
December 23	Lady Next Door
December 24	Littmann's
December 24	Lady Next Door
December 24	Scrooge [Probably A Christmas Carol broadcast]
December 25	Children's Hour
December 26	Wheatenaville
December 27-30	(Bayville Theatre)
December 28	Five Star
December 28	Lady Next Door
December 29	Household
December 29	(audition)
December 30	Lady Next Door
December 30	Records
December 30	Littmann's

1933

January 1	Children's Hour
January 3	(audition)
January 4	Records
January 5	Wheatenaville
January 6	Lady Next Door
January 7	Lady Next Door
January 8	Children's Hour
January 9	Lady Next Door
January 11	Lady Next Door
January 11	Wayside Cottage
January 13	Lady Next Door
January 13	March of Time

January 14	Lady Next Door
January 15	Children's Hour
January 16	Lady Next Door
January 17	Wheatenaville
January 17	Lucky Strike
January 18	Lady Next Door
January 18	Wheatenaville
January 18	(audition)
January 19	Lady Next Door
January 19	Wheatenaville
January 20	Lady Next Door
January 21	Helen & Mary [The Adventures of Helen & Mary]
January 22	Children's Hour
January 23	Lady Next Door
January 23	(audition)
January 24	(audition)
January 24	(audition)
January 25	Lady Next Door
January 25	(audition)
January 26	Lady Next Door
January 26	(audition)
January 27	(audition)
January 28	Lady Next Door
January 29	Children's Hour
January 30	Lady Next Door
February 1	Lady Next Door
February 4	Helen & Mary
February 4	Lady Next Door
February 5	Children's Hour
February 6	Lady Next Door
February 7	(audition)
February 7	Wheatenaville
February 8	Lady Next Door
February 9	(audition)
February 10	Lady Next Door
February 10	(Katonah Fire Company) [P.A. in New York]

February 11	(Pathe)
February 12-20	(audition Socony.)
February 12	Children's Hour
February 13	Licoln Prairie
February 15	Lady Next Door
February 16	The Great Jeasper
February 17	Lady Next Door
February 17	(audition)
February 19	Children's Hour
February 20	Lady Next Door
February 21	Wheatenaville
February 23	Lady Next Door
February 23	Wheatenaville
February 24	(audition)
February 25	Helen & Mary
February 25	Lady Next Door
February 26	Children's Hour
February 26	Sloan's
February 27	Lady Next Door
February 27	Wheatenaville
March 1	Lady Next Door
March 2	Wheatenaville
March 3	Lady Next Door
March 3	March of Time
March 4	Lady Next Door
March 4	(pictures) [Probably publicity photo session]
March 5	Children's Hour
March 6	Records
March 6	Lady Next Door
March 7	Lady Next Door
March 8	Buck Rogers
March 9	Buck Rogers
March 10	Socony Vac.
March 12	Children's Hour
March 14	Lady Next Door
March 16	Lady Next Door
March 18	Lady Next Door

March 19	Children's Hour
March 19	(Mrs. Seeley)
March 19	Big Ben
March 20	Lady Next Door
March 21	Lady Next Door
March 21	(audition)
March 22	Household
March 25	Lady Next Door
March 26	Children's Hour
March 26	Sloan's
March 27	Lady Next Door
March 28	Lady Next Door
March 30	Lady Next Door
March 31	Records
March 31	Lady Next Door
April 1	Helen & Mary
April 1	Lady Next Door
April 2	Children's Hour
April 3	Lady Next Door
April 3	(audition)
April 3	Household
April 4	Lady Next Door
April 5	Lady Next Door
April 8	Helen & Mary
April 8	Lady Next Door
April 8	Neighbors
April 9	Children's Hour
April 10	Lady Next Door
April 11	Listerine
April 12	American School of the Air
April 12	Listerine
April 13	Records
April 13	Jack and the Beanstalk
April 14	Jack and the Beanstalk
April 15	Lady Next Door
April 15	Neighbors
April 16	Children's Hour
April 17	Lady Next Door

April 17	Blind Asylum [Probably a P.A. benefit]
April 18	Lady Next Door
April 18	Raising Jr.
April 19	(Jewish home) [Benefit]
April 20	Lady Next Door
April 22	Lady Next Door
April 22	Helen & Mary
April 22	(audition)
April 22	Black Beauty
April 23	Children's Hour
April 24	(audition)
April 25	Lady Next Door
April 26	(audition)
April 27	Morse Code
April 28	Bayside Orphan Asylum [Benefit]
April 29	Helen & Mary
April 29	Lady Next Door
April 30	Children's Hour
May 2	Lady Next Door
May 5	Socony Vac. [Socony-Vacuum Corporation program AKA Seconyland]
May 6	Lady Next Door
May 7	Children's Hour
May 8	(audition)
May 8	(audition)
May 9	Lady Next Door
May 10	(audition)
May 11	Lady Next Door
May 13	Lady Next Door
May 14	Children's Hour
May 18	Lady Next Door
May 19	(audition)
May 20	Lady Next Door
May 20	Square Club
May 21	Children's Hour
May 22	(audition)
May 22	(audition)
May 23	Lady Next Door

May 23	(audition)
May 23	(audition)
May 25	Lady Next Door
May 27	Lady Next Door
May 27	(Ned Wayburn)
May 28	Children's Hour
May 29	Lady Next Door
May 30	Lady Next Door
June 2	Socony Vac.
June 2	(audition)
June 3	Lady Next Door
June 4	Children's Hour
June 5	(audition)
June 6	Lady Next Door
June 6	(audition)
June 7	(audition)
June 8	(audition)
June 8	Lady Next Door
June 9	(audition)
June 10	Helen & Mary
June 10	Lady Next Door
June 11	Children's Hour
June 12	(audition)
June 13	(audition)
June 17	Lady Next Door
June 17	(Ned Wayburn)
June 18	Children's Hour
June 19	Radio Guild
June 21	(audition)
June 21	Winnie the Pooh
June 23	Winnie the Pooh
June 23	Robinson
June 24	Lady Next Door
June 25	Children's Hour
June 25	Page of Romance
June 26	Lady Next Door
June 26	(audition)
June 27	Lady Next Door

June 28	Lady Next Door
June 29	Lady Next Door
June 29	(audition)
July 1	Lady Next Door
July 1	Helen & Mary
July 2	Children's Hour
July 3	Lady Next Door
July 5	Winnie the Pooh
July 8	Helen & Mary
July 8	Lady Next Door
July 9	Children's Hour
July 10	Drake's Drums
July 10	Soconyland
July 11	Lady Next Door
July 11	Rex Cole
July 12	Lady Next Door
July 12	Winnie the Pooh
July 12	Stephen Foster
July 14	Winnie the Pooh
July 15	Lady Next Door
July 17	(audition)
July 17	(audition)
July 17	Drake's Drums
July 18	(audition)
July 18	Lady Next Door
July 19	Winnie the Pooh
July 19	Stephen Foster
July 20	Lady Next Door
July 20	(Pathe)
July 21	(test)
July 22	Lady Next Door
July 22	(audition)
July 23	Children's Hour
July 24	Records
July 25	Lady Next Door
July 25	(audition)
July 26	Lady Next Door
July 26	(audition)

July 27	Lady Next Door
July 29	Lady Next Door
August 1	Lady Next Door
August 2	(audition)
August 3	Lady Next Door
August 4	(audition)
August 6	Children's Hour
August 7	(audition)
August 7	(audition)
August 7	(audition)
August 7	Lady Next Door
August 8	Lady Next Door
August 8	(audition)
August 8	(audition)
August 9	(audition)
August 9	(audition)
August 9	(audition)
August 12	Lady Next Door
August 13	Children's Hour
August 14	Lady Next Door
August 15	Lady Next Door
August 16	(audition)
August 17	Lady Next Door
August 19	Lady Next Door
August 20	Children's Hour
August 21	Drake's Drums
August 22	(audition)
August 23	Lady Next Door
August 23	(audition)
August 23	(audition)
August 24	Show Boat
August 27	Children's Hour
August 28	Lady Next Door
August 28	Drake's Drums
August 29	Lady Next Door
August 30	Lady Next Door
August 31	Lady Next Door
August 31	(audition)

September 2	The Sun
September 3	Children's Hour
September 5	Lady Next Door
September 5	(audition)
September 5	Rex Cole
September 6	Lady Next Door
September 7	Krakts
September 8	Hellmann's
September 9	Lady Next Door
September 10	Children's Hour
September 12	Lady Next Door
September 12	Eno
September 13	Eno
September 13	(audition)
September 14	(audition)
September 16	Hellmann's
September 17	Children's Hour
September 18	Lady Next Door
September 20	Lady Next Door
September 21	Lady Next Door
September 21	(audition)
September 22	(audition)
September 24	Children's Hour
September 24	Main Street
September 24	Miss Willie Bird
September 26	Lady Next Door
September 27	Lady Next Door
September 28	Show Boat
September 30	Lady Next Door
October 1	Children's Hour
October 2	Main Street
October 2	Lady Next Door
October 3	Buck Rogers (2 shows)
October 4	Main Street
October 4	Buck Rogers (2 shows)
October 5	(audition)
October 5	Buck Rogers (2 shows)
October 6	Hellmann's

October 8	Children's Hour
October 8	Main Street
October 9	Buck Rogers (2 shows)
October 10	Buck Rogers (2 shows)
October 11	Buck Rogers (2 shows)
October 11	Main Street
October 12	Buck Rogers (2 shows)
October 13	Hellmann's
October 14	Lady Next Door
October 15	Children's Hour
October 15	Big Ben
October 15	Main Street
October 16	Buck Rogers (2 shows)
October 16	Lady Next Door
October 17	American Legend
October 17	Buck Rogers (2 shows)
October 18	Buck Rogers (2 shows)
October 18	Lady Next Door
October 18	Main Street
October 19	Buck Rogers (2 shows)
October 20	Hellmann's
October 21	Lady Next Door
October 22	Children's Hour
October 22	Main Street
October 23	Buck Rogers (2 shows)
October 23	Lady Next Door
October 24	Buck Rogers (2 shows)
October 25	Buck Rogers (2 shows)
October 25	Main Street
October 26	Buck Rogers (2 shows)
October 26	Lady Next Door
October 26	Hellmann's
October 28	Lady Next Door
October 29	Children's Hour
October 29	Gilbert's
October 29	Main Street
November 1	Main Street
November 2	(audition)

November 3	(audition)
November 5	Children's Hour
November 5	Big Ben
November 5	Main Street
November 6	Buck Rogers (2 shows)
November 6	Lady Next Door
November 7	Buck Rogers (2 shows)
November 8	Lady Next Door
November 8	Buck Rogers (2 shows)
November 8	Main Street
November 9	Buck Rogers (2 shows)
November 10	Hellmann's
November 12	Children's Hour
November 12	Gilbert's
November 12	Main Street
November 15	The Wizard of Oz
November 17	Lady Next Door
November 18	Lady Next Door
November 19	Children's Hour
November 19	Gilbert's
November 19	Main Street
November 20	The Wizard of Oz
November 21	Eno
November 22	The Wizard of Oz
November 22	(audition)
November 23	(audition)
November 24	The Wizard of Oz
November 25	Lady Next Door
November 26	Children's Hour
November 26	Gilbert's
November 26	Main Street
November 27	Lady Next Door
November 27	The Wizard of Oz
November 29	The Wizard of Oz
November 29	Main Street
November 29	Louise M. Olcott [Louisa May Alcott]
November 30	Lady Next Door
December 1	The Wizard of Oz

December 2	Records
December 2	Lady Next Door
December 3	Children's Hour
December 3	Gilberts
December 3	Main Street
December 4	The Wizard of Oz
December 4	Lady Next Door
December 6	Lady Next Door
December 6	Main Street
December 7	Wheatenaville
December 8	Records
December 9	Lady Next Door
December 10	Children's Hour
December 10	Gilberts
December 10	Main Street
December 11	Lady Next Door
December 11	Gilberts
December 13	Main Street
December 14	Easy Aces
December 14	Records
December 14	Gilberts
December 15	Easy Aces
December 15	Wheatenaville
December 16	Gilberts
December 16	Lady Next Door
December 17	Children's Hour
December 17	Main Street
December 19	Easy Aces
December 19	Lady Next Door
December 20	Easy Aces
December 20	Lady Next Door
December 20	Main Street
December 21	Easy Aces
December 21	Underwood
December 22	Easy Aces
December 23	Helen & Mary
December 24	Children's Hour
December 24	Bar X [Bobby Benson's Adventures]

December 24	Col. Drama Guild
December 25	Pragant of Christ [Pageant of Christ]
December 26	Buck Rogers (2)
December 30	Helen & Mary
December 30	Lady Next Door
December 31	Children's Hour

1934

January 3	Lady Next Door
January 3	Wheatenaville
January 4	Fred Allen
January 6	Motor Dame
January 6	Major Andrews
January 7	Children's Hour
January 7	Bar X
January 9	Tattered Man
January 10	Lady Next Door
January 10	Castoria
January 12	Lady Next Door
January 13	Lady Next Door
January 14	Children's Hour
January 14	Bar X
January 14	Cream of Wheat
January 16	Tattered Man
January 17	Lady Next Door
January 18	Wheatenaville
January 20	Lady Next Door
January 21	Children's Hour
January 21	Bar X
January 21	Hall of Fame
January 22	Lady Next Door
January 23	Buck Rogers (2)
January 24	Buck Rogers (2)
January 25	Buck Rogers (2)
January 26	Lady Next Door
January 28	Children's Hour
January 28	Jack Benny (2)
January 29	Buck Rogers (2)

January 30	Tattered Man
February 1	Lady Next Door
February 3	Helen & Mary
February 4	Children's Hour
February 4	Cream of Wheat
February 5	Lady Next Door
February 5	Big Show
February 7	Lady Next Door
February 7	Dickens Pregent [Pageant]
February 8	Lady Next Door
February 9	(St. Georges Soc.)
February 11	Children's Hour
February 11	Big Ben
February 11	Irene Rich [Irene Rich Dramas]
February 12	American School of the Air
February 12	Buck Rogers (2 shows)
February 13	Lady Next Door
February 13	Buck Rogers (2 shows)
February 14	Buck Rogers (2 shows)
February 15	Lady Next Door
February 16	Maud Adams
February 18	Children's Hour
February 22	Winnie the Pooh
February 22	Wheatenaville
February 22	Show Boat
February 23	Maud Adams
February 24	Records
February 25	Children's Hour
February 26	(Records)
February 26	Lady Next Door
February 27	Tattered Man
February 28	Conoco
March 1	Lady Next Door
March 1	Winnie the Pooh
March 2	Maud Adams
March 3	Helen & Mary
March 3	Lady Next Door
March 3	Ripley's

March 4	Children's Hour
March 5	Lady Next Door
March 6	Lady Next Door
March 6	Tattered Man
March 6	(audition)
March 7	(audition)
March 8	Lady Next Door
March 10	Helen & Mary
March 11	Children's Hour
March 12	Lady Next Door
March 13	Lady Next Door
March 13	Tattered Man
March 14	Fred Allen (2)
March 15	Show Boat (2)
March 17	Helen & Mary
March 18	Children's Hour
March 19	Soconyland
March 20	Lady Next Door
March 22	Ford
March 24	Helen & Mary
March 25	Children's Hour
March 26	Minnevitch
March 29	Lady Next Door
March 31	Helen & Mary
March 31	Fox Col.
April 1	Bar X
April 2	Lady Next Door
April 3	Minnevitch
April 4	Wheatenaville
April 4	(Lady MacKenzie)
April 5	Lady Next Door
April 5	Show Boat (2)
April 7	(audition)
April 8	Children's Hour
April 9	Lady Next Door
April 9	Big Show
April 10	Minnevitch [P.A. with Borah Minnevich & His Harmonica Rascals]

April 10	Camel's
April 11	Lady Next Door
April 11	Castoria
April 14	Helen & Mary
April 14	Bard of Erin
April 14	Lady Next Door
April 15	Children's Hour
April 17	Lady Next Door
April 18	Fred Allen (2)
April 19	Lady Next Door
April 20	(audition)
April 21	Helen & Mary
April 21	Lady Next Door
April 22	Children's Hour
April 22	Cream of Wheat
April 25	Lady Next Door
April 25	Cuckoo [The Cuckoo Hour]
April 26	Ford
April 28	Helen & Mary
April 28	Lady Next Door
April 29	Cream of Wheat
April 30	Lady Next Door
April 30	(audition)
May 3	Buck Rogers (2)
May 5	Helen & Mary
May 6	Children's Hour
May 6	Freddy Rich
May 7	Lady Next Door
May 7	Buck Rogers (2)
May 7	Radio Guild
May 8	Buck Rogers (2)
May 9	Cuckoo
May 10	Lady Next Door
May 12	Helen & Mary
May 13	Children's Hour
May 13	Rose & Drums [Civil War stories]
May 14	Buck Rogers (2)
May 14	Tasty Yeast

May 15	Buck Rogers (2)
May 16	Lady Next Door
May 16	Buck Rogers (2)
May 17	Lady Next Door
May 19	Let's Pretend
May 19	Lady Next Door
May 20	Children's Hour
May 21	Buck Rogers (2)
May 22	Buck Rogers (2)
May 23	Buck Rogers (2)
May 26	Let's Pretend
May 27	Children's Hour
May 27	45 Min. Hollywood [45 Minutes from Hollywood]
May 28	Buck Rogers (2)
May 29	Buck Rogers (2)
May 29	Lady Next Door
May 30	Buck Rogers (2)
May 31	Buck Rogers (2)
June 1	Al. Orchester
June 2	Let's Pretend
June 2	Lady Next Door
June 3	Children's Hour
June 3	45 Min. Hollywood
June 4	Buck Rogers (2)
June 4	Lady Next Door
June 4	(audition)
June 5	Buck Rogers (2)
June 6	Buck Rogers (2)
June 7	Buck Rogers (2)
June 9	Let's Pretend
June 10	Children's Hour
June 12	Buck Rogers (2)
June 13	Buck Rogers (2)
June 14	Buck Rogers (2)
June 14	Show Boat (2)
June 15	Certo
June 16	Let's Pretend

June 16	Lady Next Door
June 16	(Abam & Strass) [Abraham & Strauss was large New York department store]
June 17	Children's Hour
June 18	Buck Rogers (2)
June 19	Buck Rogers (2)
June 20	Buck Rogers (2)
June 20	Fred Allen (2)
June 21	Show Boat (2)
June 23	Let's Pretend
June 24	Children's Hour
June 26	Tasty Yeast
June 27	Fred Allen (2)
June 28	Winnie the Pooh
June 28	Show Boat (2)
June 29	Ai. of Orch.
August 18	Lady Next Door
August 19	Children's Hour
August 22	Fred Allen (2)
August 25	Let's Pretend
August 25	Lady Next Door
August 26	Children's Hour
August 28	Lady Next Door
August 29	Lady Next Door
August 29	Fred Allen (2)
August 30	Bar X
September 1	Let's Pretend
September 1	Lady Next Door
September 2	Children's Hour
September 8	Let's Pretend
September 8	Lady Next Door
September 9	Children's Hour
September 12	Fred Allen (2)
September 12	Fred Allen Com.
September 13	(audition)
September 13	Wheatenaville
September 14	Lady Next Door
September 14	(audition)

September 15	Let's Pretend
September 16	Children's Hour
September 17	Lady Next Door
September 18	Buck Rogers (2)
September 19	Buck Rogers (2)
September 19	Fred Allen (2)
September 19	Fred Allen Com. (2)
September 20	Buck Rogers (2)
September 20	Wheatenaville
September 21	True Story (2)
September 22	Let's Pretend
September 23	Children's Hour
September 24	Buck Rogers
September 24	Wheatenaville
September 25	Buck Rogers (2)
September 25	(audition)
September 26	While Owl
September 29	Let's Pretend
September 30	Children's Hour
October 1	Big Show
October 3	(audition)
October 5	Records
October 6	True Story (2)
October 7	Children's Hour
October 7	Vicks
October 7	Joe Penner
October 9	Records
October 9	Eno
October 9	Lady Next Door
October 10	Lady Next Door
October 10	Eno
October 11	Steel
October 13	Let's Pretend
October 14	Children's Hour
October 14	Jack Benny (2)
October 15	Buck Rogers (2)
October 16	Buck Rogers (2)
October 17	Buck Rogers (2)

October 17	Fred Allen (2)
October 18	Buck Rogers (2)
October 18	Wheatenaville
October 19	Gilberts (Thrills of Tomorrow premiere)
October 20	Let's Pretend
October 20	Romberg
October 21	Children's Hour
October 23	Palmoliver
October 24	Fred Allen (2)
October 24	American School of the Air
October 25	Liberty
October 25	Buck Rogers (2)
October 26	Gilberts
October 26	March of Time
October 27	Let's Pretend
October 27	Lady Next Door
October 29	Buck Rogers (2)
October 30	Records
October 31	American School of the Air
October 31	Wheatenaville
November 2	Gilberts
November 3	Let's Pretend
November 3	Lady Next Door
November 4	Children's Hour
November 5	Wheatenaville
November 7	American School of the Air
November 7	Fred Allen (2)
November 8	45 Min. Hollywood
November 9	Gilberts
November 10	Let's Pretend
November 11	Children's our
November 11	Vicks
November 12	Martins
November 13	Buck Rogers (2)
November 13	Records
November 14	Buck Rogers (2)
November 14	American School of the Air
November 14	Fred Allen (2)

November 14	Fred Allen Com. (2)
November 15	Lady Next Door
November 16	Gilberts
November 17	Let's Pretend
November 17	Lady Next Door
November 17	Roxy [The Roxy Revue]
November 17	(Naval Lodge Mason)
November 18	Children's Hour
November 18	Heart Thobs [Heart Throbs of the Hills]
November 19	Buck Rogers (2)
November 20	Buck Rogers (2)
November 21	American School of the Air
November 22	(audition)
November 22	Lady Next Door
November 23	Gilberts
November 24	Let's Pretend
November 24	Lady Next Door
November 25	Children's Hour
November 26	Lady Next Door
November 27	American School of the Air
November 28	American School of the Air
November 30	Gilberts
December 1	Let's Pretend
December 1	Romberg
December 2	Children's Hour
December 4	Geo. Givot [Variety show]
December 5	American School of the Air
December 6	Show Boat
December 7	Gilberts
December 8	Let's Pretend
December 8	Lady Next Door
December 9	Children's Hour
December 9	Vicks
December 9	Jack Benny (2)
December 12	American School of the Air
December 12	Fred Allen (2)
December 14	American School of the Air
December 14	Gilberts

December 15	Let's Pretend
December 15	Lady Next Door
December 16	Children's Hour
December 17	(audition)
December 19	American School of the Air
December 19	Fred Allen (2)
December 22	Let's Pretend
December 22	Romberg
December 23	Children's Hour
December 23	Vicks
December 23	Jack Benny (2)
December 23	Walter Winchell (2) [Walter Winchell's Jergens Journal]
December 25	Palmoliver
December 27	45 Min. Hollywood
December 29	Let's Pretend
December 29	Lady Next Door
December 30	Children's Hour
December 31	Records

1935

January 2	Buck Rogers (2)
January 3	Wheatenaville
January 3	Fords
January 5	Let's Pretend
January 5	Lady Next Door
January 6	Children's Hour
January 6	Vicks
January 7-9	(auditions)
January 10	Lady Next Door
January 12	Let's Pretend
January 13	Children's Hour
January 14	Lady Next Door
January 15	Dark Enchantment
January 16	American School of the Air
January 16	Records
January 17	Records
January 18	Lady Next Door

January 19	Let's Pretend
January 20	Children's Hour
January 21	Lady Next Door
January 22	Dark Enchantment
January 23	American School of the Air
January 23	Fred Allen (2)
January 23	Lady Next Door
January 24	Lady Next Door
January 24	Liberty
January 26	Let's Pretend
January 27	Joe Penner
January 27	Children's Hour
January 29	Lady Next Door
January 30	American School of the Air
February 2	Let's Pretend
February 3	Children's Hour
February 6	American School of the Air
February 6	Lady Next Door
February 9	Let's Pretend
February 9	Roxy
February 10	Children's Hour
February 11	Lady Next Door
February 13	American School of the Air
February 13	Lady Next Door
February 15	March of Time
February 16	Let's Pretend
February 16	Mickey of the Circus
February 17	Children's Hour
February 17	Eddie Cantor
February 19	Lady Next Door
February 20	American School of the Air
February 20	Fred Allen (2)
February 22	Wheatenaville
February 23	Let's Pretend
February 24	Children's Hour
February 26	Lady Next Door
February 26	Bobbie Benson
February 27	American School of the Air

February 27	Fred Allen (2)
February 28	Bobbie Benson
March 1	American School of the Air
March 1	Bobbie Benson
March 2	Let's Pretend
March 3	Lady Next Door
March 3	Children's Hour
March 4	Bobbie Benson
March 5	Lady Next Door
March 5	Bobbie Benson
March 6	American School of the Air
March 6	Bobbie Benson
March 6	Fred Allen (2)
March 7	Housekeeping
March 7	Bobbie Benson
March 7	Show Boat
March 8	Bobbie Benson
March 9	Let's Pretend
March 10	Children's Hour
March 11	Bobbie Benson
March 12	(audition)
March 12	Bobbie Benson
March 13	American School of the Air
March 13	Bobbie Benson
March 14	(Astoria Church) [P.A. Astoria Presbyterian Church in NY]
March 15	Bobbie Benson
March 16	Let's Pretend
March 17	Children's Hour
March 17	Joe Penner [The Baker's Broadcast]
March 18	Bobbie Benson
March 19	Lady Next Door
March 19	Bobbie Benson
March 19	(audition)
March 20	Bobbie Benson
March 20	American School of the Air
March 21	Bobbie Benson
March 21	Show Boat

March 22	Bobbie Benson
March 23	Let's Pretend
March 23	Lady Next Door
March 24	Children's Hour
March 24	Man. Merry Go Round [Manhattan Merry-Go-Round]
March 25	Bobbie Benson
March 26	Lady Next Door
March 26	Records
March 27	American School of the Air
March 28	Show Boat
March 30	Let's Pretend
March 30	Lady Next Door
March 31	Children's Hour
March 31	Lux
March 31	Man. Merry Go Round
April 1	Records
April 1	Bobbie Benson
April 2	Records
April 2	Bobbie Benson
April 2	Lady Next Door
April 3	American School of the Air
April 3	Fred Allen (2)
April 5	(Prof. School)
April 5	Bobbie Benson
April 6	Let's Pretend
April 6	Lady Next Door
April 7	Children's Hour
April 8	Bobbie Benson
April 8	Records
April 9	Records
April 9	Bobbie Benson
April 10	American School of the Air
April 10	Bobbie Benson
April 11	Bobbie Benson
April 12	Bobbie Benson
April 13	Let's Pretend
April 13	Lady Next Door

April 14	Children's Hour
April 15	Records
April 15	Bobbie Benson
April 16	Records
April 16	Lady Next Door
April 17	American School of the Air
April 17	Bobbie Benson
April 17	Buck Rogers (2)
April 18	Bobbie Benson
April 18	Buck Rogers (2)
April 19	Bobbie Benson
April 20	Records
April 20	Lady Next Door
April 21	Children's Hour
April 22	Records
April 22	Buck Rogers (2)
April 22	Bobbie Benson
April 23	Buck Rogers (2)
April 23	Records
April 23	Lady Next Door
April 25	Bobbie Benson
April 26	Bobbie Benson
April 27	Let's Pretend
April 27	Lady Next Door
April 27	(audition)
April 27	Socony [Snow Village Sketches]
April 28	Children's Hour
April 29	Records
April 29	Bobbie Benson
April 30	Records
April 30	(audition)
May 1	American School of the Air
May 1	Bobbie Benson
May 1	Fred Allen (2)
May 2	Bobbie Benson
May 3	Bobbie Benson
May 4	Let's Pretend
May 4	Lady Next Door

May 5	Children's Hour
May 6	Bobbie Benson
May 7	Bobbie Benson
May 7	Lady Next Door
May 7	(audition)
May 8	American School of the Air
May 8	Bobbie Benson
May 8	Fred Allen (2)
May 9	(audition)
May 11	Let's Pretend
May 11	Lady Next Door
May 12	Children's Hour
May 16	(Christ Church)
May 17	(audition)
May 18	Lady Next Door
May 18	Records
May 19	Children's Hour
May 19	Joe Penner
May 20	Buck Rogers (2)
May 20	Bobbie Benson
May 21	Records
May 21	Buck Rogers (2)
May 21	Bobbie Benson
May 22	Buck Rogers (2)
May 23	Buck Rogers (2)
May 23	Records
May 25	Let's Pretend
May 25	Lady Next Door
May 26	Children's Hour
May 27	Buck Rogers (2)
May 29	Buck Rogers (2)
May 30	Buck Rogers (2)
May 31	Bobbie Benson
June 1	Let's Pretend
June 2	Children's Hour
June 2	Joe Penner
June 3	Buck Rogers (2)
June 5	Buck Rogers (2)

June 5	Fred Allen (2)
June 6	Buck Rogers (2)
June 8	Let's Pretend
June 9	Children's Hour
June 10	Buck Rogers (2)
June 11	Buck Rogers (2)
June 12	Buck Rogers (2)
June 13	Buck Rogers (2)
June 14	(audition)
June 15	Let's Pretend
June 15	(Ridgefield Pk. Pol)
June 16	Children's Hour
June 17	Buck Rogers (2)
June 18	Buck Rogers (2)
June 19	Buck Rogers (2)
June 20	(audition)
June 20	Buck Rogers (2)
June 22	Let's Pretend
June 22	(U.S. Amb. Assn.)
June 22	Lady Next Door
June 23	Children's Hour
June 24	Buck Rogers (2)
June 25	Buck Rogers (2)
June 26	Buck Rogers (2)
June 27	Buck Rogers (2)
June 29	Atlantic City
June 30	Joe Penner
July 1	Buck Rogers (2)
July 1	(audition)
July 2	Simpson Boys [Simpson Boys of Sprucehead Bay]
July 2	Buck Rogers
July 3	Buck Rogers
July 3	Simpson Boys
July 5	Records
July 5	Winnie the Pooh
July 6	Let's Pretend
July 6	Lady Next Door

July 7	Children's Hour
July 7	Star Dust [Variety program]
July 9	(audition)
July 9	Winnie the Pooh
July 10	Simpson Boys
July 13	Let's Pretend
July 13	Lady Next Door
July 14	Children's Hour
July 15	Buck Rogers (2)
July 16	Simpson Boys
July 16	Buck Rogers (2)
July 17	Simpson Boys
July 17	Buck Rogers (2)
July 18	Better Housing
July 18	(audition)
July 18	Buck Rogers (2)
July 20	Lady Next Door
July 21	Children's Hour
July 22	Alice Orchestila
July 23	Winnie the Pooh
July 24	(audition)
July 24	(audition)
July 24	Buck Rogers (2)
July 25	MacBeth
July 25	Buck Rogers (2)
July 27	Simpson Boys
July 28	Children's Hour
July 29	Buck Rogers
July 30	Simpson Boys
July 30	Winnie the Pooh
July 31	Simpson Boys
August 1	Simpson Boys
August 1	Winnie the Pooh
August 1	Show Boat
August 3	Let's Pretend
August 6	Simpson Boys
August 6	Records
August 7	(Records)

August 10	Let's Pretend
August 10	Lady Next Door
August 12	Lambardo Roard [Possibly on the road with Guy Lombardo]
August 13	Simpson Boys
August 14	Kate Smith
August 14	(audition)
August 16	(audition)
August 17	Let's Pretend
August 18	Children's Hour
August 22	Simpson Boys
August 22	Lady Next Door
August 23	Simpson Boys
August 24	Let's Pretend
August 24	Lady Next Door
August 25	Children's Hour
August 25	Ray Perkins
August 27	Records
August 27	Records
August 31	Let's Pretend
August 31	Lady Next Door
September 2	Lambardo Road
September 3	Lady Next Door
September 3	March of Time
September 5-7	(Worchester, Mass.)
September 10	(audition)
September 12	Show Boat
September 13	March of Time
September 13	(audition)
September 14	Let's Pretend
September 14	Lady Next Door
September 15	Children's Hour
September 16	(audition)
September 18	(audition)
September 19	Show Boat
September 20	March of Time
September 21	Let's Pretend
September 22	Children's Hour

September 22	Lady Next Door
September 23	(audition)
September 25	(audition)
September 26	Show Boat
September 28	Let's Pretend
September 29	Children's Hour
September 30	Lambardo Road
September 30	Lux
October 1	(audition)
October 2	March of Time
October 3	Show Boat
October 5	Let's Pretend
October 5	Simpson Boys
October 6	Children's Hour
October 8	Simpson Boys
October 8	Helen Hayes (2)
October 9	Simpson Boys
October 10	Show Boat
October 11	Simpson Boys
October 12	Let's Pretend
October 13	Children's Hour
October 15	Helen Hayes (2)
October 16	Simpson Boys
October 16	(audition)
October 17	Simpson Boys
October 18	Simpson Boys
October 19	Let's Pretend
October 20	Children's Hour
October 22	Simpson Boys
October 22	American School of the Air
October 22	Buck Rogers (2)
October 22	Helen Hayes (2)
October 23	Simpson Boys
October 23	American School of the Air
October 24	Simpson Boys
October 23	Cavalcade [Cavalcade of America "The Spirit of Competition"]
October 25	Simpson Boys

October 26	Let's Pretend
October 26	Simpson Boys
October 26	Lady Next Door
October 27	Children's Hour
October 28	Buck Rogers (2)
October 28	Lambardo Road
October 28	Andrew Carnegie
October 29	Buck Rogers (2)
October 29	Helen Hayes (2)
October 30	American School of the Air
October 30	Buck Rogers (2)
October 30	Bobbie Benson
October 30	Fred Allen (2)
October 31	Buck Rogers (2)
November 1	Bobbie Benson
November 1	Pamoliver
November 2	Let's Pretend
November 4	Bobbie Benson
November 4	Lambardo Road
November 5	Helen Hayes (2)
November 6	Simpson Boys
November 6	American School of the Air
November 6	Bobbie Benson
November 7	Buck Rogers (2)
November 8	Bobbie Benson
November 9	Let's Pretend
November 10	Children's Hour
November 11	Buck Rogers (2)
November 11	Bobbie Benson
November 11	Lambardo Road
November 11	Andrew Carnegie
November 12	Simpson Boys
November 12	American School of the Air
November 12	Buck Rogers (2)
November 12	Helen Hayes (2)
November 13	American School of the Air
November 13	Buck Rogers (2)
November 13	Bobbie Benson

November 14	Buck Rogers (2)
November 14	March of Time
November 15	Bobbie Benson
November 16	Let's Pretend
November 16	Lady Next Door
November 17	Children's Hour
November 17	(Quality Street)
November 18	Bobbie Benson
November 19	Helen Hayes (2)
November 20	American School of the Air
November 22	Bobbie Benson
November 23	Let's Pretend
November 24	Children's Hour
November 25	Bobbie Benson
November 27	American School of the Air
November 27	Bobbie Benson
November 27	Fred Allen (2)
November 29	Bobbie Benson
November 29	March of Time
November 30	Let's Pretend
November 30	Mark Twain
December 1	Children's Hour
December 1	Funnies
December 2	Bobbie Benson
December 2	(audition)
December 2	March of Time
December 3	March of Time
December 4	American School of the Air
December 4	Bobbie Benson
December 5	Home Town
December 5	Show Boat
December 6	Simpson Boys
December 6	Bobbie Benson
December 8	Children's Hour
December 8	Funnies
December 9	Bobbie Benson
December 10	Helen Hayes
December 11	American School of the Air

December 11	Bobbie Benson
December 11	Buck Rogers (2)
December 12	Show Boat
December 12	Buck Rogers (2)
December 13	Bobbie Benson
December 14	Let's Pretend
December 14	Lady Next Door
December 15	Children's Hour
December 15	Funnies
December 15	Terhune (2)
December 16	Bobbie Benson
December 16	Buck Rogers (2)
December 17	Buck Rogers (2)
December 18	American School of the Air
December 18	Bobbie Benson
December 18	Fred Allen (2)
December 18	Ipana (2)
December 19	(audition)
December 19	Show Boat
December 20	Bobbie Benson
December 20	Eternal Question
December 21	Let's Pretend
December 22	Children's Hour
December 22	Funnies
December 23	Bobbie Benson
December 24	Simpson Boys
December 24	Helen Hayes (2)
December 24	Visit of St. Nick
December 25	Bobbie Benson
December 25	Cavalcade [Cavalcade of America "The Juvenile Court Story"]
December 25	Fred Allen (2)
December 25	Ipana (2)
December 26	Simpson Boys
December 27	Bobbie Benson
December 28	Let's Pretend
December 28	Lady Next Door
December 29	Children's Hour

December 29	Funnies
December 30	Bobbie Benson
December 31	Helen Hayes (2)

1936

January 1	Col. Drama Guild
January 1	Bobbie Benson
January 2	March of Time
January 3	Bobbie Benson
January 4	Let's Pretend
January 5	Children's Hour
January 5	Funnies
January 5	Echoes of New York
January 6	Bobbie Benson
January 8	Bobbie Benson
January 8	American School of the Air
January 8	March of Time
January 9	Show Boat
January 10	Bobbie Benson
January 11	Let's Pretend
January 12	Children's Hour
January 12	Funnies
January 13	Bobbie Benson
January 14	Helen Hayes (2) ["The New Penny"]
January 14	(audition)
January 15	American School of the Air
January 15	Bobbie Benson
January 15	Fred Allen (2)
January 16	Show Boat
January 17	Bobbie Benson
January 18	Let's Pretend
January 19	Children's Hour
January 19	Funnies
January 20	Bobbie Benson
January 20	(audition)
January 20	(audition)
January 20	Col. Drama Guild
January 22	American School of the Air

January 22	Bobbie Benson
January 23	Show Boat
January 24	Buck Rogers (2)
January 24	Bobbie Benson
January 25	Let's Pretend
January 26	Children's Hour
January 26	Funnies
January 27	Buck Rogers (2)
January 27	Bobbie Benson
January 29	American School of the Air
January 29	Buck Rogers (2)
January 29	Bobbie Benson
January 29	Fred Allen (2)
January 30	News of Youth
January 30	Show Boat
January 31	Buck Rogers (2)
January 31	Bobbie Benson
February 1	Let's Pretend
February 2	Children's Hour
February 2	Funnies
February 2	Eddie Cantor
February 3	Buck Rogers (2)
February 3	Bobbie Benson
February 4	News of Youth
February 5	Simpson Boys
February 5	American School of the Air
February 5	Buck Rogers (2)
February 5	Bobbie Benson
February 6	News of Youth
February 7	Buck Rogers (2)
February 7	Bobbie Benson
February 7	March of Time
February 7	(audition)
February 8	Let's Pretend
February 8	News of Youth
February 9	Children's Hour
February 9	Echoes of New York
February 10	Bobbie Benson

February 10	Buck Rogers (2)
February 11	Records
February 12	Buck Rogers (2)
February 12	Bobbie Benson
February 14	Buck Rogers (2)
February 14	Bobbie Benson
February 15	Let's Pretend
February 15	Lady Next Door
February 15	News of Youth
February 16	Children's Hour
February 16	Funnies
February 17	Simpson Boys
February 17	Bobbie Benson
February 18	Helen Hayes (2)
February 19	American School of the Air
February 19	Bobbie Benson
February 19	Fred Allen (2)
February 20	News of Youth
February 21	Bobbie Benson
February 25	News of Youth
February 26	American School of the Air
February 26	Dreams of Long Ago (2)
February 27	Show Boat
February 28	Buck Rogers (2)
February 29	Let's Pretend
February 29	Records
February 29	News of Youth
March 1	Children's Hour
March 1	Funnies
March 2	Buck Rogers (2)
March 4	American School of the Air
March 4	Buck Rogers (2)
March 4	Fred Allen (2)
March 5	Show Boat
March 6	Buck Rogers (2)
March 6	March of Time
March 7	Let's Pretend
March 7	Palmolive (2)

March 8	Echoes of New York
March 9	Buck Rogers (2)
March 10	Helen Hayes (2)
March 11	American School of the Air
March 11	Buck Rogers (2)
March 13	Buck Rogers (2)
March 14	Let's Pretend
March 15	Children's Hour
March 15	Funnies
March 18	Simpson Boys
March 18	American School of the Air
March 18	Fred Allen (2)
March 19	Show Boat
March 21	Let's Pretend
March 22	Children's Hour
March 22	Funnies
March 22	Echoes of New York
March 25	American School of the Air
March 25	March of Time
March 28	Let's Pretend
March 29	Children's Hour
March 29	Funnies
April 1	Fred Allen (2)
April 1	American School of the Air
April 4	Let's Pretend
April 5	Children's Hour
April 5	Funnies
April 8	American School of the Air
April 8	Fred Allen (2)
April 8	March of Time
April 9	Show Boat
April 11	Let's Pretend
April 12	Children's Hour
April 12	Funnies
April 13	Simpson Boys
April 15	Fred Allen (2)
April 16	Death Valley Days
April 18	Let's Pretend

April 19	Children's Hour
April 20	Bobbie Benson
April 22	American School of the Air
April 22	Bobbie Benson
April 23	News of Youth
April 24	Bobbie Benson
April 25	News of Youth
April 26	Children's Hour
April 26	Funnies
April 26	Echoes of New York
April 26	Paul Whiteman (2)
April 28	News of Youth
April 29	American School of the Air
April 29	(audition)
May 1	(Newburg, NY)
May 2	(Newburg, NY)
May 3	Children's Hour
May 3	Paul Whiteman (2)
May 5	News of Youth
May 7	Show Boat (2)
May 9	Let's Pretend
May 10	Children's Hour
May 10	Funnies
May 10	Paul Whiteman (2)
May 12	News of Youth
May 13	Fred Allen (2)
May 14	News of Youth
May 15	Bobbie Benson
May 16	Let's Pretend
May 16	News of Youth
May 17	Children's Hour
May 17	Funnies
May 18	(audition)
May 20	(Lady MacKenzie)
May 21	Death Valley Days
May 23	Let's Pretend
May 23	News of Youth
May 24	Children's Hour

May 24	Funnies
May 26	News of Youth
May 26	(audition)
May 27	Cavalcade [Cavalcade of America "Resourcefulness"]
May 28	Records
May 28	News of Youth
May 30	Let's Pretend
May 31	Children's Hour
May 31	Funnies
June 3	(audition)
June 4	Records
June 4	News of Youth
June 5	(christening of boat)
June 6	Let's Pretend
June 6	News of Youth
June 6	(Peekskill) [P.A. in NY]
June 7	Children's Hour
June 7	Funnies
June 10	Fred Allen (2)
June 10	Ipana (2)
June 11	Records
June 11	News of Youth
June 13	Let's Pretend
June 13	News of Youth
June 14	Children's Hour
June 20	Let's Pretend
June 20	News of Youth
June 21	Children's Hour
June 21	Funnies
June 24	Gang Busters
June 27	Let's Pretend
June 27	News of Youth
June 28	Children's Hour
June 28	Funnies
July 1	(audition)
July 2	News of Youth
July 5	Children's Hour

July 5	Radio Album
July 6	Bobbie Benson
July 7	News of Youth
July 8	Bobbie Benson
July 9	News of Youth
July 9	Death Valley Days
July 11	Let's Pretend
July 12	Children's Hour
July 12	Funnies
July 14	News of Youth
July 15	Gang Busters
July 16	News of Youth
July 17	(audition)
July 18	Let's Pretend
July 19	Children's Hour
July 19	Funnies
July 21	(audition)
July 21	News of Youth
July 23	News of Youth
July 24	(audition)
July 24	(audition)
July 25	News of Youth
July 25	Let's Pretend
July 26	Funnies
July 26	Feen-A-Mint
July 27	(audition, FoxyGr. PA)
July 28	(audition, Hoople)
July 28	(audition, Foxy)
July 28	News of Youth
July 29	Renfrew (2) [Renfrew of the Mounted Police – Tales of the Canadian Mounted Police]
July 29	March of Time
July 30	Renfrew (2)
July 31	Renfrew (2)
August 1	Let's Pretend
August 1	News of Youth
August 2	Children's Hour

August 2	Funnies
August 3	Renfrew (2)
August 4	News of Youth
August 4	Renfrew (2)
August 4	March of Time [Documentary-type program]
August 5	Old Dr. Jim [Probably daily soap opera]
August 5	Renfrew (2)
August 6	Renfrew (2)
August 6	Death Valley Days
August 8	Let's Pretend
August 10	Old Dr. Jim
August 10	(audition, McK. & Jor.)
August 11	Old Dr. Jim
August 11	News of Youth
August 12	Cavalcade [Cavalcade of America "Concert Band Comes to Town"]
August 13	News of Youth
August 14	Old Dr. Jim
August 15	Let's Pretend
August 15	News of Youth
August 16	Children's Hour
August 16	Funnies
August 17	(rehearsal, Phil. Lord)
August 18	(rehearsal, Phil. Lord)
August 18	News of Youth
August 20	(audition, Phil. Lord)
August 20	News of Youth
August 22	News of Youth
August 23	Children's Hour
August 23	Funnies
August 24	Home Sweet Home [Daily serial]
August 25	News of Youth
August 26	(audition, McK. & Jor.)
August 26	Town Hall (2) [Town Hall Tonight with Fred Allen]
August 27	Records
August 27	News of Youth

August 28	March of Time
August 30	Children's Hour
August 30	Funnies
September 8	News of Youth
September 10	News of Youth
September 12	Let's Pretend
September 13	Children's Hour
September 13	Funnies
September 15	News of Youth
September 16	Gang Busters
September 19	Let's Pretend
September 19	News of Youth
September 20	Children's Hour
September 20	Funnies
September 21	March of Time
September 22	News of Youth
September 24	News of Youth
September 26	Let's Pretend
September 26	Workshop
September 27	Children's Hour
September 27	Funnies
September 28	Jack Masters [Treasure Adventures of Jack Masters]
September 29	News of Youth
September 30	Jack Masters
October 2	Jack Masters
October 4	Children's Hour
October 4	Funnies
October 5	Renfrew (2)
October 5	Jack Masters
October 7	Jack Masters
October 7	Fred Allen (2)
October 8	Kate Smith [Variety show with dramatic sequence]
October 9	Jack Masters
October 10	News of Youth
October 11	Children's Hour
October 11	Funnies

October 12	Jack Masters
October 12	Helen Hayes (2)
October 13	News of Youth
October 14	Jack Masters
October 14	American School of the Air
October 15	News of Youth
October 16	Jack Masters
October 17	News of Youth
October 18	Children's Hour
October 18	Funnies
October 18	We the People ["Human interest" stories]
October 19	Jack Masters
October 21	American School of the Air
October 21	Jack Masters
October 21	Fred Allen (2)
October 22	Kate Smith
October 23	Jack Masters
October 24	Let's Pretend
October 24	News of Youth
October 25	Children's Hour
October 25	Funnies
October 26	Jack Masters
October 27	News of Youth
October 28	Jack Masters
October 29	News of Youth
October 30	Jack Masters
October 30	Welch [Irene Rich Dramas sponsored by Welch Grape Juice]
October 31	Let's Pretend
October 31	Barn Show
November 1	Children's Hour
November 1	Funnies
November 1	Magic Key [Variety show AKA The Magic Key of RCA]
November 2	Jack Masters
November 4	American School of the Air
November 4	Jack Masters
November 4	Gang Busters

November 5	March of Time
November 6	Jack Masters
November 7	Let's Pretend
November 8	Children's Hour
November 8	Funnies
November 9	Jack Masters
November 11	Fred Allen (2)
November 11	Jack Masters
November 13	Jack Masters
November 14	Let's Pretend
November 15	Funnies
November 16	Jack Masters
November 18	American School of the Air
November 18	Jack Masters
November 18	Renfrew (2)
November 19	Renfrew (2)
November 20	Jack Masters
November 20	Renfrew (2)
November 20	True Story (2)
November 22	Children's Hour
November 23	Jack Masters
November 25	American School of the Air
November 25	Easy Aces
November 25	Jack Masters
November 26	Kate Smith [Kate Smith A&P Bandwagon]
November 27	Jack Masters
November 28	Let's Pretend
November 28	News of Youth
November 29	Children's Hour
November 29	Funnies
November 30	Jack Masters
December 2	American School of the Air
December 2	Jack Masters
December 2	Records (2)
December 3	Billy & Betty [Children's show with Billy & Betty White]
December 3	Kate Smith

December 4	Jack Masters
December 4	Billy & Betty
December 5	Let's Pretend
December 5	Barn Show
December 6	Children's Hour
December 6	Funnies
December 7	Jack Masters
December 7	Billy & Betty
December 8	Billy & Betty
December 9	American School of the Air
December 9	Jack Masters
December 10	Billy & Betty
December 11	Jack Masters
December 11	Billy & Betty
December 11	(Clan MacKenzie)
December 12	Let's Pretend
December 12	Barn Show
December 13	Children's Hour
December 13	Capt. Diamond [Captain Diamond's Ads]
December 13	Echoes of New York
December 14	Jack Masters
December 14	Billy & Betty
December 15	Billy & Betty
December 16	American School of the Air
December 16	Billy & Betty
December 16	Jack Masters
December 16	Fred Allen (2)
December 17	Billy & Betty
December 18	Jack Masters
December 18	Records
December 19	Let's Pretend
December 19	Thornton Fisher
December 20	Funnies
December 20	Children's Hour
December 21	Jack Masters
December 21	Helen Hayes New Penny (2) [Helen Hayes Theater "New Penny"]

December 23	Jack Masters
December 23	Fred Allen (2)
December 24	Christmas Party [P.A.]
December 24	Dicken's A Christmas Carol
December 25	Jack Masters
December 25	Toyland [Probably one-time Christmas show]
December 26	Let's Pretend
December 26	Barn Show
December 27	Children's Hour
December 27	Funnies
December 30	Gang Busters
December 31	March of Time

1937

January 1	Col. Dram.
January 2	Let's Pretend
January 3	Children's Hour
January 3	Funnies
January 4	Billy & Betty
January 5	Billy & Betty
January 6	Billy & Betty
January 7	Billy & Betty
January 7	Bert Lahr
January 8	Billy & Betty
January 9	Let's Pretend
January 9	Barn Show
January 10	Children's Hour
January 10	Funnies
January 11	Billy & Betty
January 11	Helen Hayes (2)
January 13	American School of the Air
January 13	Billy & Betty
January 14	Floyd Gibbins [Colgate True Adventure]
January 15	Billy & Betty
January 16	Let's Pretend
January 17	Children's Hour
January 17	Funnies

January 20	Fred Allen (2)
January 22	Records
January 23	Barn Show
January 23	(Kearney, New Jersey)
January 24	Children's Hour
January 24	Funnies
January 24	Capt. Diamond
January 24	Echoes of New York
January 25	Billy & Betty
January 26	Billy & Betty
January 27	American School of the Air
January 27	Billy & Betty
January 27	Fred Allen (2)
January 29	Billy & Betty
January 30	Let's Pretend
January 31	Children's Hour
January 31	Funnies
January 31	Echoes of New York
February 1	Warden Laws
February 3	Billy & Betty
February 4	Billy & Betty
February 5	News of Youth
February 6	Let's Pretend
February 6	Shell Show
February 7	Children's Hour
February 7	Funnies
February 8	(audition)
February 9	(audition)
February 10	American School of the Air
February 10	News of Youth
February 12	Singing Lady
February 13	Let's Pretend
February 13	Barn Show
February 13	Joe Cook [Circus Night in Silvertown]
February 14	Children's Hour
February 15	(audition)
February 17	American School of the Air
February 19	(audition)

February 19	News of Youth
February 20	Let's Pretend
February 20	Barn Show
February 20	Joe Cook
February 21	Children's Hour
February 21	Funnies
February 22	News of Youth
February 24	American School of the Air
February 24	News of Youth
February 24	Fred Allen (2)
February 25	Hy Brown [Probably an audition for writer/director/producer Hi Brown]
February 26	News of Youth
February 27	Let's Pretend
February 27	Barn Show
February 28	Children's Hour
February 28	Funnies
March 1	News of Youth
March 3	American School of the Air
March 3	News of Youth
March 3	Fred Allen (2)
March 5	News of Youth
March 6	Let's Pretend
March 6	Barn Show
March 6	Joe Cook
March 8	News of Youth
March 10	American School of the Air
March 10	News of Youth
March 12	News of Youth
March 12	Death Valley Days
March 13	Let's Pretend
March 13	Barn Show
March 14	Children's Hour
March 14	Funnies
March 15	News of Youth
March 15	Billy & Betty
March 16	Billy & Betty
March 17	American School of the Air

March 17	News of Youth
March 19	News of Youth
March 20	Let's Pretend
March 20	Barn Show
March 20	Joe Cook
March 21	Children's Hour
March 21	Funnies
March 21	Work Shop
March 22	Billy & Betty
March 24	American School of the Air
March 25	Billy & Betty
March 26	March of Time
March 27	Let's Pretend
March 28	Funnies
March 31	Fred Allen (2)
April 2	Radio Guild
April 3	Let's Pretend
April 4	Children's Hour
April 4	Funnies
April 6	Billy & Betty
April 7	American School of the Air
April 7	Billy & Betty
April 8	Records
April 10	Let's Pretend
April 10	Barn Show
April 10	Joe Cook
April 11	Children's Hour
April 11	Funnies
April 14	American School of the Air
April 14	Fred Allen (2)
April 15	Records
April 16	Geo. Rector
April 17	Let's Pretend
April 17	Barn Show
April 18	Children's Hour
April 18	Funnies
April 21	American School of the Air
April 22	Radio Music Hall

April 23	David Harum [Daily soap opera]
April 24	Let's Pretend
April 24	Barn Show
April 25	Children's Hour
April 25	Funnies
April 26	Ma & Pa [Serial drama]
April 27	Ma & Pa
April 28	David Harum
April 28	American School of the Air
April 28	Ma & Pa
April 29	Records
April 29	Ma & Pa
April 30	David Harum
April 30	Ma & Pa
May 1	Let's Pretend
May 1	Joe Cook
May 2	Children's Hour
May 2	Funnies
May 2	Bert Lahr [Comedy/variety program]
May 3	(audition)
May 3	Ma & Pa
May 4	Ma & Pa
May 5	David Harum
May 5	(audition)
May 5	Ma & Pa
May 6	Ma & Pa
May 7	Records
May 7	Ma & Pa
May 8	Let's Pretend
May 8	Snow Village [Sketches]
May 9	Children's Hour
May 9	Funnies
May 10	Ma & Pa
May 11	Ma & Pa
May 13	Billy & Betty
May 13	Floyd Gibbins
May 15	Let's Pretend
May 15	Barn Show

May 16	Children's Hour
May 16	Funnies
May 17	Ma & Pa
May 18	Billy & Betty
May 19	Billy & Betty
May 20	Geo. Rector
May 20	Billy & Betty
May 22	Let's Pretend
May 22	Barn Show
May 22	(Warners) [Possibly P.A. at one of the Warners theaters]
May 23	Children's Hour
May 23	Funnies
May 26	Ma & Pa
May 26	Fred Allen (2)
May 27	Ma & Pa
May 28	Records
May 28	Ma & Pa
May 28	Death Valley Days
May 29	Let's Pretend
May 29	Wyandote Players
May 30	Children's Hour
May 31	Billy & Betty
May 31	Ma & Pa
June 2	Gang Busters
June 4	(audition)
June 5	Let's Pretend
June 5	Barn Show
June 6	Children's Hour
June 6	Echoes of New York
June 7	Ma & Pa
June 8	Billy & Betty
June 8	Ma & Pa
June 9	Peggy Wood
June 9	Fred Allen (2)
June 11	Billy & Betty
June 11	Log Cabin R [The Jack Haley Show AKA Log Cabin Jamboree]

June 11	King Tot R
June 11	Aunt Mary R
June 12	Let's Pretend
June 13	Children's Hour
June 13	Funnies
June 13	Work Shop
June 15	Billy & Betty
June 19	Let's Pretend
June 19	Barn Show
June 20	Children's Hour
June 20	Work Shop
June 20	Sealtest
June 24	Peter Pan
June 26	Let's Pretend
June 26	Barn Show
June 26	(audition)
June 27	Children's Hour
July 3	Let's Pretend
July 3	Barn Show
July 4	Children's Hour
July 4	Braves of Brave
July 4	Sealtest
July 5	Billy & Betty
July 6	Billy & Betty
July 7	Town Hall (2)
July 10	Let's Pretend
July 10	Barn Show
July 11	Children's Hour
July 13	Billy & Betty
July 15	Log Cabin R
July 24	Let's Pretend
July 24	Barn Show
July 25	Children's Hour
July 25	Sealtest
July 28	Town Hall (2)
July 29	March of Time
August 1	Sealtest
August 4	Town Hall (2)

August 9	Billy & Betty
August 10	(audition)
August 11	Town Hall (2)
August 16	Log Cabin R
August 19	March of Time
August 21	Let's Pretend
August 22	Sealtest
August 23	Killy Kelly (2) [NBC soap opera Kitty Kelley]
August 25	Town Hall (2)
August 28	Let's Pretend
August 28	Barn Show
August 29	Children's Hour
August 29	Dreams of Long Ago
September 1	Town Hall (2)
September 1	Commercial (2)
September 4	Let's Pretend
September 4	Barn Show
September 5	Children's Hour
September 9	March of Time
September 10	Log Cabin R
September 11	Let's Pretend
September 11	Barn Show
September 12	Children's Hour
September 12	(off to Hollywood)
September 29	Texaco (2)
October 5	Packard (2) [Variety hour with Fred Astaire]
October 6	Texaco
October 25	Grape Nut (2)
October 25	Commercial (2)
November 11	Maxwell House (2)
November 17	Town Hall (2)
November 18	Maxwell House
November 16	Packard (2)
November 24	Fred Allen (2)
December 1	Fred Allen (2)
December 7	Packard (2)

December 8	Fred Allen (2)
December 15	Fred Allen (2)
December 21	Big Town (2)
December 22	Fred Allen (2)
December 29	Fred Allen (2)
December 29	Wops
December 30	Wops

1938

January 5	Wops
January 6	Wops
January 22	Jack Haley (2)
January 23	Jean Hersholt [Dr. Christian]
January 28	Texaco (2)
February 1	Packard (2)
February 9	Texaco (2)
February 14	Texaco (2)
February 20	Hollywood Playhouse (2)
March 1	Big Town (2)
March 16	Hollywood Parade
April 3	The Mickey Mouse Theatre of the Air

Other Radio Credits

December 9, 1938	Big Town
February 7, 1939	Fibber McGee and Molly
February 21, 1939	Fibber McGee and Molly
March 20, 1939	Lux Radio Theatre ("It Happened One Night" with Clark Gable and Claudette Colbert)
June 11, 1939	Radio Guild
March 17, 1940	The Campbell Playhouse
October 15, 1940	Fibber McGee and Molly
December 29, 1940	Jack Benny
February 5, 1941	It's Time to Smile
May 16, 1941	The Great Gildersleeve (audition)
August 31, 1941 –	The Great Gildersleeve

March 21, 1957	
October 20, 1941	Lux Radio Theatre ("Blood and Sand" with Tyrone Power and Annabella)
November 15, 1941	NBC's Fifteenth Anniversary Party
1942	This Is My Best ("Around the World in Eighty Days" with Orson Welles)
July 23, 1942	Command Performance (with Pat O'Brien, Frances Langford, Alfred Newman & the 20th Century Fox Studio Orchestra, Hal "Gildersleeve" Peary, Lillian "Birdie" Randolph, Cab Calloway Orchestra)
November 10, 1942	The George Burns and Gracie Allen Show
September 18, 1943	Command Performance – (with Ronald Colman, Jascha Heifetz, Rise Stevens, Lena Horne, Robert Benchley, 43rd Army Air Forces Band, Gardner Field Band)
February 18, 1943	The Bob Burns Show
April 1, 1943	The Bob Burns Show
April 8, 1943	The Bob Burns Show
April 22, 1943	The Bob Burns Show
May 2, 1943	The Bob Burns Show
May 6, 1943	The Bob Burns Show
May 20, 1943	The Bob Burns Show
June 17, 1943	The Bob Burns Show
December 2, 1943	Suspense
February 23, 1944	Radio Almanac
March 1, 1944	Radio Almanac
April 27, 1944	Suspense
June 15, 1944	The Dinah Shore Program
June 15, 1944	Birdseye Open House (with Phil Harris)

November 16, 1944	Suspense ("Dead of the Night" with Robert Cummings)
November 21, 1944	This Is My Best
February 8, 1945	Suspense
April 18, 1945	Mail Call
November 8, 1945	Command Performance
1945	The Anderson Family
March 18, 1946	The Harry Von Zell Show (audition; with Frank Nelson)
August 8, 1946	Suspense
September 29, 1946 – June 18, 1954	The Phil Harris/Alice Faye Show
October 14, 1946	The Cavalcade of America
November 4, 1946	The Cavalcade of America
November 12, 1946	Fibber McGee and Molly
1947	The Anderson Family (several)
February 14, 1947	The Alan Young Show
March 9, 1947	The Fitch Bandwagon
July 13, 1947	The Jack Paar Show
July 24, 1947	Family Theater ("Brass Buttons" with Maureen O'Hara, Regis Toomey)
October 21, 1947	Here's To Veterans
January 8, 1948	Family Theater ("The Happiest Person in the World" with William Bendix)
March 30, 1948	Fibber McGee and Molly
April 10, 1948	The Kid on the Corner (audition; with Sheldon Leonard)
April 25, 1948	The Fitch Bandwagon
May 23, 1948	Guest Star
December 25, 1948	Command Performance (with Cass Daley, Jerry Colonna, Frank Nelson, Mel Blanc, Francis X. Bushman, Donald Crisp, William Conrad, Jeffrey Silver and Jane Webb)
October 26, 1950	Suspense

March 22, 1951	Screen Directors' Playhouse ("The Great Lover" with Bob Hope and Rhonda Fleming)
September 26, 1952	Cascade of Stars (with Groucho Marx, Judy Canova, etc.)
June 2, 1953	Fibber McGee and Molly
December 30, 1953	Crime Classics ("Coyle and Richardson: Why They Hung In A Spanking Breeze")
January 6, 1954	Crime Classics ("The Younger Brothers: Why Some Of Them Grew No Older")
April 13, 1954	Fibber McGee and Molly
May 17, 1954	Fibber McGee and Molly
January 13, 1958	You Bet Your Life (promo spot for NBC)
February 13, 1972	Same Time, Same Station (Rebroadcast of early shows)
November 26, 1973	The Hollywood Radio Theatre
November 27, 1973	The Hollywood Radio Theatre
November 28, 1973	The Hollywood Radio Theatre
November 29, 1973	The Hollywood Radio Theatre
November 30, 1973	The Hollywood Radio Theatre

Misc. Undated Radio Appearances

Substituted for Johnny, the Philip Morris call boy
Mail Call (episode #141 with Hal Peary)

Films

1938	Sally, Irene and Mary (20th Century-Fox)
1938	A Trip to Paris (20th Century-Fox; The Jones Family series)
1938	Lord Jeff (MGM)
1938	Prairie Moon (Republic)

1939	You Can't Cheat an Honest Man (Universal)
1939	They Shall Have Music (United Artists)
1939	Tower of London (Universal)
1939	The Spirit of Culver (Universal)
1939	The Family Next Door (Universal)
1939	Boy Slaves (RKO)
1940	Emergency Squad (Paramount)
1940	Framed (Universal)
1940	Under Texas Skies (Republic)
1940	The Villain Still Pursued Her (RKO)
1940	Military Academy (Columbia)
1940	Let's Make Music (RKO)
1941	Ride, Kelly, Ride (20th Century-Fox)
1941	The Haunted Mouse (Warner Brothers; cartoon)
1941	Horror Island (Universal)
1941	Out of the Fog (Warner Brothers)
1942	Sing Your Worries Away (RKO)
1942	Broadway (Universal)
1942	Invisible Agent (Universal)
1942	The Pride of the Yankees (RKO)
1942	A Yank at Eaton (MGM)
1942	Who Done It? (Universal)
1942	Thunder Birds (20th Century-Fox)
1942	Moonlight in Havana (Universal)
1942	Gorilla Man (Warner Brothers)
1942	Eyes in the Night (MGM)
1943	Mystery Broadcast (Republic)
1943	Fish Fry (Universal; Andy Panda cartoon)
1943	Gildersleeve on Broadway (RKO)
1943	The Painter and the Pointer (Universal; Andy Panda cartoon)
1944	The Lodger (20th Century-Fox)
1944	Her Primitive Man (Universal)
1944	Pin-Up Girl (20th Century-Fox)
1944	Follow the Boys (Universal)
1944	Casanova Brown (RKO)
1944	Bowery to Broadway (Universal)

1945	I'll Remember April (Universal)
1945	Molly and Me (20th Century-Fox)
1945	It's in the Bag! (United Artists)
1945	Crow Crazy (Universal; Andy Panda cartoon)
1946	How Do You Do? (PRC)
1946	Apple Andy (Universal; Andy Panda cartoon)
1946	Mousie Came Home (Universal; Andy Panda cartoon)
1946	The Wacky Weed (Universal; Andy Panda cartoon)
1948	The Playful Pelican (Universal; Andy Panda cartoon)
1949	Scrappy Birthday (Universal; Andy Panda cartoon)

Television

1949-52	Pantomime Quiz
1957	The Woody Woodpecker Show (Andy Panda)
1961	The Bullwinkle Show (Sherman)
1967	George of the Jungle
1969	The Dudley Do-Right Show

Index